The Disciple Making Church

By Bill Hull:

Jesus Christ Disciplemaker
The Disciple Making Pastor
Can We Save the Evangelical Church?
The Disciple Making Church

The
Disciple
Making
Church

Bill Hull

Fleming H. Revell
A Division of Baker Book House Co
Grand Rapids, Michigan 49516

TO Howard Ball,
my philosophical mentor, who taught me
how to make disciples for local churches.
Thanks, Howard!

Unless otherwise identified, Scripture quotations are from the Holy Bible: New International Version. Copyright © 1973, 1978, 1984 International Bible Society. Used by permission of Zondervan Bible Publishers.

Verses marked TLB are taken from *The Living Bible*, Copyright © 1971 by Tyndale House Publishers, Wheaton, Ill. Used by permission.

Scripture quotations identified NAS are from the New American Standard Bible, © The Lockman Foundation 1960, 1962, 1963, 1968, 1971, 1972, 1973, 1975, 1977.

The Scripture quotations contained herein identified RSV are from the Revised Standard Version of the Bible, Copyrighted © 1946, 1952, 1971, by the Division of Christian Education of the National Council of the Churches of Christ in the United States of America, and are used by permission. All rights reserved.

Library of Congress Cataloging-in-Publication Data

Hull, Bill, date
   The disciple making church / Bill Hull.
      p.   cm.
   ISBN 0-8007-1641-8
   1. Discipling (Christianity)   I. Title.
BV4520.H78   1990
253—dc20   90-35377
                                   CIP

Copyright © 1990 by Bill Hull
Published by Fleming H. Revell
a division of Baker Book House Company
P.O. Box 6287, Grand Rapids, MI 49516-6287
All rights reserved.

Sixth printing, November 1994

Printed in the United States of America

CONTENTS

Foreword

Bill Hull understands the frustrations, fears, and hopes of church leaders everywhere, as they hunger to see their churches become what Scripture reveals they should be and history verifies they once were. *The Disciple making Church* completes Bill Hull's *Jesus Christ Disciplemaker* and *The Disciple Making Pastor* and rounds out his remarkable contribution to the Lord's church around the world. These books are a powerful expression of Bill's competency in the Bible, theological training, pastoring experience, and passion for the potential of churches everywhere. Here is mature and practical understanding for putting your church on the path that leads to discipling-church growth and that most treasured commentary from the Lord: "Well done, good and faithful servant."

HOWARD BALL
President of Churches Alive

Introduction
Is Disciple Making for Everyone?

At one of my seminars, a pastor seated in the third row raised his hand. "I like your emphasis on discipling," he commented when I called on him. "But it isn't for everyone.

"I think you are right that Jesus modeled discipling principles, but I don't see it in Acts and the Epistles. After all, the word *disciple* is not used after Acts 21. The apostles must have realized the church was different. It's not practical to apply disciple making to the whole church—not everyone is interested in such things."

Though I did not agree with the man, I could appreciate how he felt. He had not responded maliciously. He had merely expressed his own angst at trying to make discipling his church's core ministry. Because he had encountered difficulties, he voiced the objections of his congregation and other frustrated colleagues. Grasping at these theological or cultural explanations, he sought a way out.

Was he right? *Is* the need for disciple making limited to a few overzealous souls? Should evangelistic organizations and small church committees take on the whole task of evangelizing the world? What place does discipling have in the contemporary church?

The Church and Discipling
Somewhat ironically, to return it to the Great Commission, today's church has required a radical movement with the sole purpose of returning the church to a serious commitment to making disciples, as Christ commanded. The pervasive, diverse movement that has arisen has no single leader, expression, or nomenclature. You may find its proponents in

parachurch organizations and the institutionalized church. Unlike the women's movement, the civil-rights movement, and other sociopolitical groups, it lacks a national umbrella organization that coordinates and provides strategies. Nor does it seek to control people, like the ill-fated shepherding program of the 1970s.

The church has seriously responded to "blue water" mission, while neglecting "in Jerusalem" or "at home" disciple making. Both foreign missions and the American church have suffered for this mistake, because "at home" disciple making is the key to world evangelism. Unhealthy churches at home lead to weak missions abroad, but when the church makes disciples at home two good things happen: Christians become healthy and reproduce, and as they multiply, the world becomes evangelized God's way.

I guess that the pastor who voiced objections to disciple making had never been exposed to the biblical foundations of discipleship as the heart of local-church ministry. He probably grew up in a church that didn't practice it and attended a seminary that didn't teach it. Fears and misconceptions about disciple making overwhelm him. He doubts he could implement what he already believes, so he conceives of discipling as a small-group ministry or one that can only take place in a parachurch organization.

In truth, almost *any* church does *some* discipling. When a pastor uses the Bible in a sermon or a teacher opens it to a Sunday-school class, the church provides the initial phases of discipling. But disciple making must go far beyond that.

Response to my previous works *Jesus Christ Disciplemaker* and *The Disciple Making Pastor* have proved to me that many pastors have a pent-up frustration concerning making disciples. As committed leaders with hearts that burn for Christ and His church, they hunger to obey the Bible and make their lives count for Him. They believe that making disciples is the Christ-commanded heart of the church. But when they seek to rise above the trivialization of local-church work, they face the challenge of convincing their congregations of disciple making's importance and of implementing a strategy that will realize their dream.

To answer the objections against disciple making as a way of life for the church, I have written *The Disciple Making Church*. I offer it to those who would make something other than disciple making the core of the local church and to those who want to learn how to make disciple making the focus of their church.

Discipling Church, Normal Church

I work from the thesis that the discipling church *is* the normal church. Disciple making is for every Christian and every church. Understand, however, that when I speak of discipling I'm talking about a broad-based principle and process rather than an event or program.

I believe the discipling church is the normal church and that disciple making is for everyone and every church because:

1. Christ instructed the church to take part in it.
2. Christ modeled it.
3. The New Testament disciples applied it.

We'll look into each of these claims in greater depth as we see how discipling can be implemented in a church. But first, why bother to make disciples?

WHY IS THE DISCIPLING ISSUE IMPORTANT?

Most church watchers today believe in a common myth that the evangelical church is growing and the liberal church is in decline. True, the liberal church had declined, but in recent years it has experienced a resurgence. On the other hand, we hear the myth that evangelicalism is in a steady growth pattern. The truth is that while certain pockets of evangelicalism *have* grown, overall the church is in a decline. Demographical data demonstrate that, since the 1940s, it has steadily dropped in respect to population growth. Between

1970 and 1975 the number of evangelicals increased, only to decline shortly thereafter. The reported revivals of the 1970s made no significant difference in the evangelical population.[1]

The liberals are dying because of doctrine, and evangelicals might well sacrifice world evangelization on the altar of tradition.

Unless the church makes making disciples its main agenda, world evangelism is a fantasy. There is no way to reproduce, multiply, and decentralize people and the Gospel without first diligently making disciples. The way we have proceeded has not produced the quality of people or the numbers of people to perform what Christ commanded.

Historically, the church has sporadically surged and declined as a result of disobedience, and the evangelical church has largely remained disobedient to the Great Commission. The refusal to consistently make disciples causes decline that leaves the church more defeated than before, and the world does not become evangelized.

However, healthy signs have appeared on the horizon: Pastors and church leaders have become excited about the discipling movement. Do we have the courage and patience to see it through? Accomplishing the task will require major structural and philosophical changes. Denominations that change their methods and cast off unproductive tradition will flourish and experience God's power, while those who insist on the status quo will die a slow, unpleasant death.

Because I believe disciple making is the only future for the church, I have set myself three goals:

1. To make discipling more acceptable to the established church.
2. To encourage pastors and church leaders to accept their biblical mandate.
3. Leadership development.

Making Discipling More Acceptable to the Established Church. I aim to open the doors wider and knock down the walls that have kept existing churches from trying disciple making. The major change involves switching from what I call the "Christocentric" discipling model to a "churchocentric" model. This difference is not a product of my fertile imagination, though I have named and described it.

In the following pages I have attempted to document the biblical transition of discipling from the Christocentric model, which relied on Christ's leadership alone, to the churchocentric model, which developed leadership within the congregation. To do so, I have considered the examples of what I have named the *first church*, the *mission church*, and *the discipling church*. My object has been to provide a scriptural apologetic for a full-bodied discipling model. When more churches consider discipling because of the model I present in this book, I will meet my goal.

Encouraging Pastors and Church Leaders to Accept Their Biblical Mandate. Because I believe the modern pastor is the key to transforming existing churches into discipling centers, I intend to provide more ammunition for leaders to use in leading others to Great Commission obedience.

When pastors attempt to transform a generic church into a discipling church, they face a major task. They can take three major tracks to guide the church through the transition:

PREACHING. The pastor can make a bigger difference faster than any other person. The "bully pulpit," as some call it, is the means of calling people to action and presenting them with God's agenda via the Word of God. I encourage pastors to use the material in here as the starting point for developing sermons that will encourage congregations to obey the Great Commission.

SMALL GROUPS. The best way to reach the most people in the most meaningful way is through the small group. It provides all the essential elements for spiritual growth. Done correctly, small-group involvement makes disciples, identifies leaders, and gives people the relationships and accountability they need.

LEADERSHIP DEVELOPMENT. Through the small group, leaders are identified and can be placed into the leadership community as apprentices.

To encourage pastors and leaders, I provide a three-tiered seminar course that offers the inspiration and know-how to make a discipling church. In it I walk pastors through one basic and two advanced seminars, over a three- to five-year period. I would like to see such seminars supplemented through local training centers composed of kindred spirits in the discipling movement, and I challenge local pastors to become the designated representatives to lead the centers. A national support network for an ongoing consultation will be necessary to sustain real change.

In the long run, sustained real change that focuses on discipling will be lay driven. Disciple-making pastors must pass on their vision and leadership to laymen who will remain in the churches after the pastors leave. Otherwise, pastoral change may kill the vision.

Evangelizing the World God's Way. Jesus left us with the Great Commission instructions to populate heaven. He came to seek and save the lost; God chose to create man, rescue him from his plight, and use men to rescue other men.

The discipling process seeks to deliver people, develop them, and deploy them into the harvest field. Making disciples is the only way to develop healthy Christians who reproduce themselves in their own home area. The leaders among the healthy, reproducing Christians may then be deployed into the Judeas, Samarias, and extended parts of our world.

Discipling leads to reproduction and finally multiplication, which are God's design and method to reach the world. Because the church has largely ignored this process, the cause of Christ has greatly suffered. I pray that the church will become more obedient, in part because of this work.

Part I

WHAT DOES
DISCIPLE MAKING MEAN?

I would encourage both those who have doubts about the need for disciple making and those who long to make it a part of their church to consider with me the biblical evidence that I believe shows discipleship should become the focus of every church. Before we can reject the idea or put it into our churches, we need to have a clear idea of what we are rejecting or developing in the congregation.

We'll look at the biblical description of a disciple, the biblical model of the disciple maker—Jesus—and how disciple making became part of the early church. Along the way we'll build a profile of both a disciple and a disciple-making church.

To reach the world with the Gospel, we need a goal and a plan of how we'll meet that goal. I believe we can find the guidelines for that in the pages of the book of Acts.

1
A Biblical Look at Discipling

The key passage to our understanding of discipleship lies in the Great Commission itself. Before He ascended to the Father, Jesus told His disciples:

> "All authority in heaven and on earth has been given to me. Therefore go and make disciples of all nations, baptizing them in the name of the Father and of the Son and of the Holy Spirit, and teaching them to obey everything I have commanded you. And surely I am with you always, to the very end of the age."
>
> Matthew 28:18–20

Despite Jesus' clear command to "make disciples," many, like the man who claimed disciple making was not for everyone, have tried to invalidate that call by arguing that the Greek word *mathetes,* translated "disciple," does not appear in the Bible after Acts 21, so the church does not need to focus on disciple making.

Though I am not a linguist, I do not believe that invalidates Jesus' call. Let me offer some observations:

1. Acts 21:16, the last New Testament use of *disciple,* occurs nearly twenty-seven years after Paul's conversion. Luke interchangeably employs *brothers, disciples,* and *people* to describe fellow Christians, not saving *disciple* for exclusive description of the twelve. I believe this word was just one way to identify a follower of Jesus Christ. Though more than thirty years had passed since Christ's ascension, *disciple* had not ceased being used to describe ordinary believers. In fact, Luke uses *brothers, Christians, disciples,* and *believers* to describe the same people.[1]

2. The above point somewhat dispels the belief that *disciple* was sacred among the church and exclusively employed to describe the twelve. However, some credence must be lent to the idea that the word had a special meaning related to the Christocentric discipling model, characterized by the master-disciple, one-on-one relationship. Rengstorf writes, "*mathetes* always implies the existence of a personal attachment which shapes the whole life of the one described as *mathetes* and which in its particularity leaves no doubt as to who is deploying the formative power."[2]

   The change to a churchocentric discipling model required a community relationship, a shared discipling among several people. Since *disciple* carried some Christocentric baggage, in his writings Paul attempted to explain the discipling process in a different way. Though Paul did not use *mathetes,* he did use *manthano* eighteen times.[3] The latter means "to learn," the verb form of *mathetes.* Though Paul did not call individuals "disciples," he called the function of their development "discipling."

3. The issue is not primarily a lexical one, because the disappearance of the word *disciple* in the Epistles has several plausible explanations. The Gospels and Acts are histor-

ical narratives, telling a story, while the Epistles are pedagogical—they are doctrinal, conveying principles and concepts.[4] Another factor to consider is the difference in background and training of the authors. Paul, the product of a Hebrew home and a Greek culture, had studied both with Gamaliel and in Greek schools. A cosmopolitan man of letters, Paul's education and background had equipped him for cross-cultural ministry and influenced his choice of words.

Paul may have had some reverence for the historical disciples or felt his cross-cultural readers could become confused by such a term. Rengstorf believed that *disciple* fell into disrepute among the Socratic-Platonic-Aristotelian philosophers and that this attitude permanently affected its use in Greek.[5] In addition the further the church expanded away from Jewish culture, the less Jewish concepts and history helped communicate the message. Paul may have simply substituted words he thought would communicate better.

4. The authors of the Epistles developed replacement words or phrases for *disciple*. Examples include *believer, brother, Christian, faithful, imitators, saints, the called.* Words used to describe function include *model, practice, train, mature,* and *example.* To describe the relationship with the world they used *ambassador, alien,* and *pilgrim.*[6]

5. The above reasons why *disciple* disappeared in the Epistles represent some educated guesses. But the reason that stands head and shoulders above the rest is not lexical at all. I believe the change came about because the church moved from a Christocentric to a churchocentric model. Over the course of thirty years, taking the principles Jesus used to lead a one-dimensional group of twelve and making them work in a multidimensional mass of thousands required transition. Though the word may have changed, the principle of discipleship was never abolished.

WHAT DOES A DISCIPLE LOOK LIKE?

To understand disciples and discipleship, let's take a look at the Great Commission, which gives us specifications or methodology for reaching the nations with the Gospel. We'll ask four questions of Matthew 28:18–20:

1. Who should be disciples?
2. Who should make disciples?
3. How long should the process last?
4. What is included in discipleship?

Who Should Be Disciples?

Technically, from the moment of spiritual birth, every Christian is a disciple. Disciples are born by the Spirit to be made into mature reproducers, as described in John 15:7–17. They are to be made in every nation; therefore every person in the church is a disciple and has the responsibility and divine ability to be what Christ desires.

The idea that only mature people are disciples and all other Christians are immature converts appears nowhere in the New Testament. God expects every believer to be a mature, reproducing disciple. Therefore any leader can confidently stand before the church and call every believer to discipleship. In fact nothing less will please God.

Each believer should remain in Christ by means of the Word and prayer, should bear fruit that includes evangelism, and walk in obedience. Then he or she will bring glory to God, experience joy, and love others. *Every* Christian is to be a disciple.

Who Should Make Disciples?

Every disciple should make disciples. Jesus gave the command to the apostles, who represented the best and worst of mankind—you might call them mankind in microcosm. Because we have the same ability and responsibility as the original disciples, every contemporary disciple is no less capable of this calling than the twelve.

Disciple making included introducing people to Christ, building them up in faith, and sending them into the harvest field. This process can be summarized by what I call the three Ds of disciple making: *Deliver them, develop them,* and *deploy them.*

Through the power of Christ we are delivered from sin; by the discipling process we are developed into mature believers; finally God deploys us into the harvest field to reach others. Some disciples will have leadership gifts, and God will call them to spearhead the disciple-making activity. Only a few are called to leadership in the corporate body, but every disciple should take part in the disciple-making process at some level.

How Long Should the Process Last?

Jesus told the disciples to make as many disciples in as many places as they could and promised He would be with them until "the very end of the age." Christ knew the mission would outlive those men, and we have not yet reached the end of the age. Therefore Jesus' instructions remain in force today as much as they did the day He issued them. Making disciples will continue until Christ comes again. The church of Jesus Christ is under orders to keep on making disciples as long as we have breath. This is the driving force and foundation of all the church is and does.

What Is Included?

With two words, *baptizing* and *teaching,* Jesus clarified the disciple-making process. Baptizing new disciples means having them publicly profess their faith. Through this one-time, public witness, they make their declaration of allegiance to Christ. Teaching, however, is a lifelong process. "Teaching them to obey everything I have commanded you" is the exact instruction (Matthew 28:20).

Where do we build the walls that separate a discipling activity from a nondiscipling activity? What can we legitimately include in discipling? Christ sets the limits: ". . . Everything I have commanded you." Everything that falls within Christ's commands and directives we can consider discipling. The Sermon on the Mount, the Upper Room discourse, the commands to pray and love one another all fall into the discipling curriculum.

Many have the false idea that discipling involves a narrow teaching of ministry skills and accumulation of Bible knowledge, but discipling is actually as broad in scope as Jesus' teachings. By including all He taught, we broaden our understanding of *discipling.*

However, even as we broaden our scope, we must not allow that to become an excuse for a lack of intention. Nor must we lose track of the need for consistent obedience: "teaching them to obey everything I have commanded you." If we have not taught obedience and encouraged it through accountability, we have not discipled.

JESUS: MODEL DISCIPLE MAKER

When Jesus told the disciples to go and make disciples of all nations, they knew what He meant: He had taught them by His example, and they understood the principles and priorities they had seen in His behavior. They were to win others to the faith and make more of what they were.[7]

Jesus modeled both a strategy and a life-style. When a disciple was fully taught, he would be like his teacher, said Jesus (Luke 6:40). So when someone asks, "Did the disciples disciple?" we can respond, "Of course they did. How could they do anything other than what Jesus taught them? They did exactly what they knew."

Some have tried to argue that Jesus had no intentional strategy. "You must be reading a different Bible from mine," I reply. If anything shows clearly in the Gospels, it is that Jesus was a man with a plan, priorities, and a goal.

Jesus had a four-phase development plan built around four key statements, each of which inaugurated a new phase of training (*see* Chart 1).

Chart 1
A Church-Centered Disciple-Making Plan

"COME AND SEE": In this formative stage, Jesus extended an invitation for people to be introduced to Him and His work.

"COME AND FOLLOW ME": This is the developmental stage, in which Jesus trained and established mature believers. He showed them how and did it with them.

"COME AND BE WITH ME": By joining correction to the developmental stage, Jesus challenged those who had leadership skills to be with Him. Out of this came the twelve—those who received a special position and authority.

"REMAIN IN ME": In the final phase, Christ expected the disciples to reproduce. He deployed them into the world to obey His command and make disciples.

We can also see Jesus' intentional strategy in His resisting the devil in the wilderness (Matthew 4:1–11); in His refusal to meet an immediate felt need at the expense of a greater, larger goal (Mark 1:38); and His statement that He acted only when the Father acted (John 5:19). Jesus took His instructions from heaven and would not be turned away from His Father's agenda.

Neither can we doubt that Jesus kept His goal in view. No less than five times did He give the disciples Great Commission statements (Matthew 28:18–20; Mark 16:15–18; Luke 24:44–49; John 20:21; Acts 1:8). Spreading the Gospel filled His thoughts even as early as His encounter with the woman at the well (John 4), when He called the fields ripe for harvest to the attention of His disciples.

Aware of the need, Jesus lamented, "The harvest is plentiful but the workers are few. Ask the Lord of the harvest, therefore, to send out workers into his harvest field" (Matthew 9:37, 38). His immediate response was to expand the worker base: "Jesus went up on a mountainside and called to him those he wanted, and they came to him. He appointed twelve —designating them apostles—that they might be with him and that he might send them out to preach" (Mark 3:13, 14).

By preparing others for greater responsibility, Jesus could multiply His influence. Five months after their calling, the twelve went out two by two, without His physical presence (Matthew 10). Later they would lead the seventy on ministry tours. But in each case they reported back to Him for evaluation and recommendation. He instilled in them a sense of accountability built on relationship as the learning process continued.

Jesus could not focus all His efforts on the seventy—it was just too large a group to deal with successfully. Instead He formed close relationships with the twelve. By focusing on a group of that size, the disciples provided a variety of personalities, gifts, and quirks, and He could teach them to work together and through differences; but the numbers would never become unmanageable. Today's disciples have discovered that a small group remains the best discipling tool.

Slowly Jesus led the disciples toward taking over His ministry, gradually releasing more and more responsibility as they moved from one stage to the next. He had selected these men on the basis of character and gifts. Already they had placed Christ before self, possessions, and even family (Luke 14:25–33), and they would willingly sacrifice and take up their mission (Luke 9:23–25). Through these dedicated few He could work, expanding the ministry in a way no one man could. This decentralization would become more relevant after His ascension and the coming of the Holy Spirit.

THE EARLY DISCIPLES' MODEL

By the kinds of churches the apostles built, we know they *did* disciple. We'll look at the three dominant examples in the Acts and the Epistles: the *first church,* at Jerusalem; the *mission church,* a conglomerate of congregations Paul planted in his first two missionary journeys; and the *discipling church,* founded at Ephesus (*see* Chart 2). The apostles' principles were *established* in the first church, *expanded* in the mission church, and *matured* in the discipling church.

Chart 2
The Earliest Churches

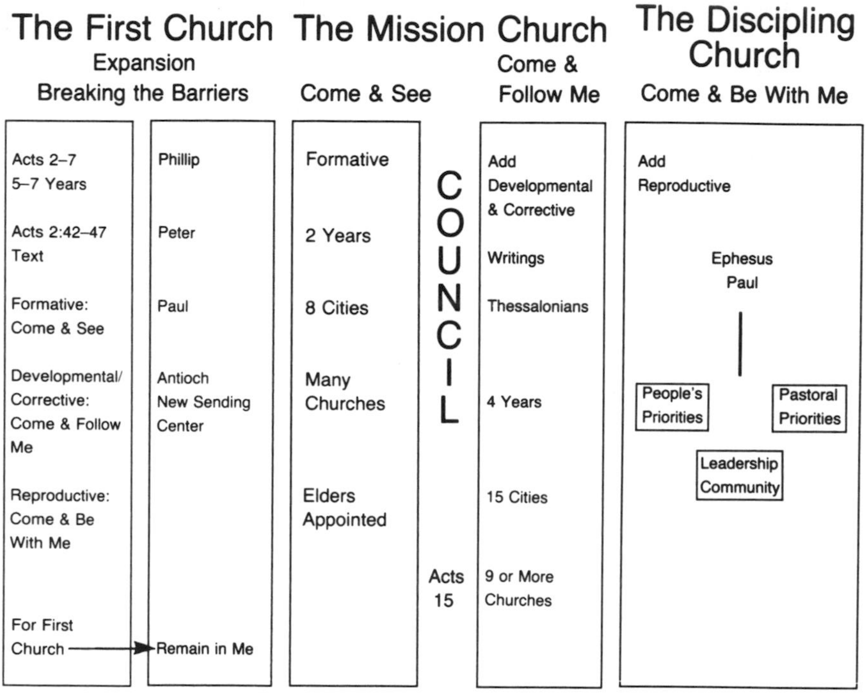

The First Church	The Mission Church	The Discipling Church
Expansion		
Breaking the Barriers	Come & See	Come & Follow Me
		Come & Be With Me

The First Church		The Mission Church			The Discipling Church		
Acts 2–7 5–7 Years	Phillip	Formative		Add Developmental & Corrective	Add Reproductive		
Acts 2:42–47 Text	Peter	2 Years		Writings		Ephesus Paul	
Formative: Come & See	Paul	8 Cities		Thessalonians			
Developmental/ Corrective: Come & Follow Me	Antioch New Sending Center	Many Churches		4 Years	People's Priorities		Pastoral Priorities
Reproductive: Come & Be With Me		Elders Appointed		15 Cities	Leadership Community		
			Acts 15	9 or More Churches			
For First Church ⟶	Remain in Me						

C O U N C I L

The First Church. In Acts 2–7 we see the initial five- to seven-year course of discipling in the first church. As Acts 2:42–47 shows, major differences between the apostles' leadership and the way Christ lead the twelve became apparent in the congregation.

> They devoted themselves to the apostles' teaching and to the fellowship, to the breaking of bread and to prayer. Everyone was filled with awe, and many wonders and miraculous signs were done by the apostles. All the believers were together and had everything in common. Selling their possessions and goods, they gave to anyone as he had need. Every day they continued to meet together in the temple courts. They broke bread in their homes and ate together with glad and sincere hearts, praising God and enjoying the favor of all the people. And the Lord added to their number daily those who were being saved.

Instead of following a Christocentric model, they began to form a churchocentric focus in the congregation. By expanding the discipling, the twelve could attain their goal: reaching the entire world for Christ.

The Mission Church. From an outpost called Antioch emerged the first major evangelistic thrust of Christianity. Two men who had not followed Christ during His earthly ministry led the way, establishing the same priorities and practices He had modeled and the apostles had applied at the first church.

Though governed by the same principles and priorities as the first church, the mission church was different. It was composed of an entire family of small churches, led by elders unknown to the mother church. The mission church affords us with an example of how churches grow and multiply; it reveals the stages of maturation churches move through and what they need as they develop. In fact churches must progress through each stage the apostles experienced under Christ's leadership. Any church that stalls will die out. Myriads of American churches have proved the truth of this as life has begun to drain away from them.

The Discipling Church. Paul spent over three years at Ephesus, and here we learn the most about the nature of a mature discipling church. We have more information about Ephesus than any other church in the New Testament, and in it we see an aggressive ministry that reached all Asia with the Gospel.

Paul's letter to the Ephesians details the people's priorities; his letters to Timothy, the pastor at Ephesus, detail pastoral priorities. Luke's account in Acts provides another look at Paul's work. From these we have a rich data base for understanding a modern version of the discipling church.

2
The Focus of the
Disciple-Making Church

In His Upper Room discourse, Jesus simultaneously gave the disciples a seminar and a warning that their relationship would never again be the same. Soon they would relate to Him through the Holy Spirit, instead of enjoying His physical presence.

When He said, ". . . It is to your advantage that I go away" (John 16:7 RSV), the disciples didn't believe it. Would we? If *we* had a choice between the physical presence of the Lord Jesus Christ and the presence of the Holy Spirit, wouldn't we take Christ? It's hard to imagine that we really *could* be better off with the Holy Spirit.

When Christ ascended, the disciples moved from the "Come and be with Me" stage into the "Remain in Me" phase of training (John 15:7). They would use the same four-point training process Jesus had taught them, but their new context required alterations in who and how many would lead the work, how the group would know God's will, how people would get trained, how outreach would be done, and the means used to meet people's needs. Though the disciples didn't like Jesus' leaving, they adapted His teachings to fit the altered circumstances.

DOES THE CHURCH NEED A CHANGE?

Much of the contemporary church has been so busy focusing on what Jesus did that it has missed the changes the apostles instituted. The enemy has used that oversight to his advantage by locking the majority of the church out of the discipling process.

In the Christocentric model, Jesus was the master and the disciples the learners. Because He was God, Jesus was enough for the twelve: He could lead them, meet every need, and develop each follower. No one had to make guesses about God's will or decide where to do outreach. Just ask Jesus.

Effective use of this model still remains in one or two small-group ministries that linger around the edge of the church and in parachurch organizations. It attracts like-minded, gifted, task-oriented people and emphasizes the accumulation of knowledge and development of ministry skills.

The Christocentric model *does* work in a group fully committed to a clear and narrow goal—such as a mission organization. The task-oriented, common-vision nature of such a group allows the model to work successfully; outreach focuses on a narrow slice of the Great Commission, unencumbered by the multiplicity of agendas and the complexity of the local church. Where all members can acquire the same skills, take the same philosophical training, and fit into one clear mission target, the model becomes effective.

In light of the overall disrepair of the evangelical church, God has graciously raised up many missions to attend to the work that needs to be done. But it does not mean we would be wise to attempt to place the parachurch philosophy into the local church. It would be like putting a square peg in a round hole.

The parachurch organization attracts a Word-oriented person, aggressive in evangelism and committed to the task—an average church probably has about 20 or 30 percent of this type in its population. The narrow Christocentric model hasn't worked in the church at large because it does not fit its variety. Most people in the local congregation are gifted in other areas, look at life through different lenses, and have a multiplicity of beliefs concerning church priorities. The Christocentric model simply cannot reach or interest enough people to become the heart of the church.

The Need for a New Model

Because the Christocentric model will not fit the needs of the church, we cannot conclude that church members need not take part in discipling. Failure to contextualize disciple making into our society and time has led to today's weak, disobedient church. Discipling should remain at the heart of the church—but it needs a multidimensional focus, one with broader applications than the church commonly accepts.

Where we have failed, the apostles acted successfully: They took the Christocentric parachurch discipling model and adapted its principles to the church. We can follow that transition through the first church, the mission church, and the discipling church. By the time Paul left Ephesus, he had forged the churchocentric model, which made a discipling church a reality.

What Is the Churchocentric Model?

In churchocentric discipling, corporate teamwork exists among the body of Christ. Outreach occurs through the different gifts of the entire church, rather than a small portion of the congregation. Though some people are verbally strong, while others play a support role, all work together for the common goal. For example, pastoral care plays a vital role in drawing people to the church and supporting them in Christ. Unless a loving, caring community exists to help newborn babes and heal the wounded, people won't come to Him or stick around long enough to be trained. Love within the community of Christ is the most powerful of all the church's evangelistic tools.

The churchocentric model recognizes the rich diversity and giftedness of the body of Christ and the way it works together as a team to create a discipling environment. When the narrow corridors of the Christocentric model are torn down and replaced by the large rooms of the churchocentric model, many who have rejected discipling as a viable church priority will take a second look.

DISCIPLING AND THE CHURCHOCENTRIC MODEL

In defining *discipling,* I have purposed to move the walls out, open the doors wider, while retaining the distinctives of discipling. Therefore I have developed this definition:

> *Discipling:* The intentional training of disciples, with accountability, on the basis of loving relationships.

Consider this definition's components:

> INTENTIONAL: Like Jesus, we must have a planned strategy. The discipling church's leadership team has a defined purpose and has thought through how to make disciples. Leadership must define *disciple,* develop a method to make disciples, and model before the congregation what a disciple is and how to make one. Passing on the vision and the know-how is important.
> TRAINING: Discipling means more than developing skills, although it must include that. *Training* implies a prescribed course of study and a process people undergo in order to reach certain goals. Small groups and other vehicles can provide a track on which people can make progress. Everyone in the congregation should receive an invitation to learn about Scripture, discover his or her gifts, and use them in Christ's service.

WITH ACCOUNTABILITY: Because people need help keeping their commitments to God, the church should provide a variety of means to hold people accountable. In fact, disciple making cannot take place without this element. A series of agreements may be made within the discipling program of the church. Both formal and informal means of accountability should be provided—everything from the buddy system to constitutional disciplinary codes.

ON THE BASIS OF LOVING RELATIONSHIPS: All successful ministry is based on relationships. The discipling church should make community building a very high priority, and all church-group life should encourage people to share their needs. A loving and supportive environment builds emotional equity that acts as a cushion during the bumps and turbulence of ministry. This emotional anchor needs to be unleashed to form the church's relational foundation.

To keep discipling effective, remember: Discipling is not an event; it is a process. No system can make a disciple, because discipleship requires that a person's will be activated by the Holy Spirit. The church has the responsibility to provide the clear vision and the vehicles that bring Christians into mature discipleship. Growth and accountability should be part of every Christian's life, for his or her entire life; the need for these doesn't end until one gets transferred to heaven.

The key to churchocentric discipling is teamwork in a loving environment that maintains the distinctives of mission, training in ministry skills, and accountability. The real evidence of success will be the constant production of reproducing disciples and leaders who become multipliers.

EFFECTIVELY USING THE CHURCHOCENTRIC MODEL IN THE CHURCH

Five major changes will be necessary for any church that wishes to move from the Christocentric into the churchocentric model. With these changes in focus, a leadership group can begin to form an effective discipling group.

1. In Leadership: Moving From Christ Leading the Apostles to Elders Leading a Congregation. If Jesus had faced the thousands at Pentecost, how would He have organized them? When it was time to expand the ministry beyond Jerusalem, how would Jesus have led the mission? Doubtless, to accomplish these tasks, He would have made some changes in the way He worked. Had He had 3,000 baptized disciples, I am convinced Jesus would have done almost exactly what the apostles did. He would have expanded the ministry to Gentiles much the way Paul did. But as long as Jesus stayed, the disciples could not fully develop, and people would have resisted their authority as long as they had Jesus to consult.

Jesus' departure gave birth to the question *Who's in charge here?* While He was on earth, the disciples argued over who would get the best celestial sky boxes and who was the greatest, but not one of the Gospels records their asking who was in charge. After His ascension, when the apostles found themselves in a stuffy room with 110 others, and a decision needed to be made, they looked at one another and began to talk. They had moved from a one-person authority base to a shared authority base.

Christ is the head of the body, but what do we do now? Paul wrote that Christ is the head of the body, and that is good theology, but when a decision has to be made, Jesus usually doesn't give instructions in an audible voice. While Christ remained on earth, authority resided in one person; after His ascension, leaders shared it. The Christocentric model is master-pupil; the churchocentric model is elders-congregation. While the Christocentric model develops an elite band of dedicated workers, the churchocentric one includes a mass of disciples at various stages, some dedicated workers, but an even larger group of the unschooled, apathetic, resistant, and seeking. In such a group discipling becomes a multidimensional task.

We could liken the distribution of church authority to a tree: Christ is the trunk; the apostles are the major limbs; elders form the smaller limbs; and members are twigs. Today Christ is ascended, and the apostles are with Him; the elders or a team of leaders are given authority to lead the church. For a group of regenerate men, filled by God's Spirit yet having feet of clay, to lead a group of disciples is far different from Christ's leading the twelve. Functionally, it requires changes in the way the church operates.

One on one is inadequate. No individual can fully disciple another, because no one has the full arsenal of spiritual gifts and wisdom to adequately bring another to maturity in Christ. That does not mean one-on-one discipling is invalid—but a master-pupil model is not enough for the church. The ministry that thinks of discipling in one-on-one terms falls short of what God intended for His people.

I need several mentors to fully develop me in Christ: a ministry-skills mentor, a character mentor, and people who will help me focus on a variety of other issues. Only the body of Christ can provide an environment that gives the full range of experiences and challenges I need. One-on-one can provide the fine-tuning in personal matters as I walk with Christ, but it cannot do the whole job.

If a church focuses only on ministry skills and one-on-one discipling, the majority of the people remain undiscipled. Many of the church's ministry needs will lie dormant, and the undiscipled will remain out of the loop. Feeling they do not have a favored status with the pastor or leaders, the people will become polarized and antagonistic. Because the Christocentric model can only reach a few, it's too narrow for the church, requires too little of the church, and makes small what God intended to be big. God's goal is that the total body fully develop the discipling church and reach the world.

What Christ was to the disciples, the leadership team is to

the congregation. The apostles led the prayers in the Upper Room. They brought the 120 from the Upper Room into the streets, to preach the Gospel, and set the agenda for the first church. After discussing and praying about the dispute over food distribution, devious giving habits, and the sticky issue of what Gentile converts would be asked to do, they provided answers. In short they provided team leadership for the first church and for Paul and guided the expansion of the mission.

These men could manage harmoniously because they agreed on the mission of the church. They had been trained by the same person, possessed a common vision, and believed in one basic methodology. Their philosophical purity made effective leadership possible. In today's church good team leadership has become rare because good training usually does not precede assuming of leadership.

Jesus had trained His disciples to be a certain kind of people, think a common way, and go about their work in a similar fashion. Yes, they had different opinions and experienced disagreements, but when it came to the task before them, they could agree and give unity to the church.

The disciples oversaw a much more diverse group than Jesus did and had to fuse together their wide variety of interests, personalities, gifts, problems, and viewpoints. After the church's rapid initial growth, twelve men had over 10,000 members to delegate authority to and manage.

Discipling means managing a system in which teaching, training, evangelism, and pastoral care take place. It involves the multidimensional work of the leadership team as they coach the congregation in a variety of ways and means. Making sure people have a ride to church and a hot meal during times of crisis is discipling, because it helps develop a person for Christ. Anything that helps a person move forward in Him fits the label *discipling.*

We must stop thinking that only Bible teaching, sharing your faith, memorizing Bible verses, and teaching ministry skills are discipling. Yes, many churches greatly neglect ministry skills, and they need to be taught, but if you have done only that, you have not discipled.

The first change from the Christocentric to churchocentric body is that one person no longer leads a small, elite band of dedicated soldiers of the cross; a leadership team coaches a multilevel, diverse congregation toward maturity in Christ.

2. In Guidance: Moving From Christ's Personal Presence to the Holy Spirit's and the Ministry of the Word, Prayer, and Others. When Jesus said, "Get in the boat so we can go over to the other side of the lake," none of His followers doubted what He wanted. Jesus' physical presence eliminated the need to discern His will. But now that He was gone, discovering His specific will became a shared experience. Jesus had the final word and the complete truth, but the apostles had neither. Instead they had His Word and enough truth to discern His will—as we do, too.

When Jesus spoke the Upper Room discourse, He gave the disciples encouragement to "remain in Me" (John 13–16). He told them they would have a new teacher, the Holy Spirit, who was like Him and would direct them into all truth (John 14:26; 16:13). Though they would not *have* all truth, they knew where to find it and the means to get it: They were to pray to the Father, in the name of Jesus, by means of the Holy Spirit (John 14:10–17).

Unlike the original disciples, we have never turned to Jesus, physically, for our answers. Instead of Christ, we have always had the Holy Spirit; instead of hearing His words, we consult the written Word; instead of eye-to-eye contact, we speak to Him in prayer. Centuries of time and the barriers of culture, language, and customs also stand between us and God's truth. Add these differences to the varied interpretations and opinions of others, and finding God's will can become difficult.

Functionally, how do we receive guidance?

We agree with God on the core data. We still have the clear words of Jesus on the core data; we know our purpose is to serve God through an obedient life-style.

We can divide that life-style into the kind of persons we are to be and the kind of task we are to pursue. In Jesus' discourse, He defined the kind of people we are to be: those who abide in Him (John 15:7–17). The task He has set us is disciple making (Matthew 28:18–20). The Scriptures erase our doubts about what living an obedient life-style means: Be disciples, make disciples.

Use what God has given for the rest. When a church's leadership team becomes disciples and places making disciples at the head of the congregation's ministry, it only needs to figure out how to create disciples. Though many consider the first part easy and the latter part difficult, I believe the opposite is true. Once the leadership team agrees on the core data and motivates people, the method, as important as it may be, becomes less critical than the belief.

But for the generic church, deciding on methodology is very difficult. Such people gather around doctrine, but not strategy, resulting in a values "free for all." Priorities and practice are up for grabs, and long, difficult sessions in which leaders try to form a policy convoy begin. Usually leaders chose the lowest-common-denominator objectives, because when someone leads into an area that cannot be agreed upon, others oppose him so rigorously that he gives up. Board meetings degenerate into struggles over territorial trivia— the fruit of the eclectic, generic church.

All this can be avoided when the church gathers around *both* doctrine and strategy. Once it has done that, methodology becomes less difficult. As good role models, leaders provide the demonstration that demands imitation and leads to reproduction. As leaders model the vision and values of the church, they lead members to obedience.

Leaders are disciples who are in touch with God. They practice what Christ preached by communicating with God through the tools of guidance: They seek God's Word for strategy, pray for guidance, and talk to one another to seek opinions from those who are cut from the same cloth. Finding

God's direction for specific ministry is a shared experience; it can be beautiful when the spiritually mature are guided by God's clear mandates and together seek to obey Him.

In the Christocentric model, one person who possesses a vision and values communicates to a like-minded membership or staff, who can execute it; Christ did not intend His church to work this way. Believe me, too—it *doesn't* work.

Christ decreed the vision and the strategy, and the president of a parachurch organization can do the same. When a pastor tries this tactic, it eventually breaks down. For quite a few years the pastor may be able to say, "God called me here and gave me the vision. You can question me, but there is a point where, if disagreement exists, you must not touch the Lord's anointed." He may even try to point out that criticizing or opposing the pastor would have been like David's opposing King Saul.

But a local pastor is not King Saul of Israel, nor does he have authority equal to that of Jesus—or even the apostles. Leadership in the church is a shared experience, and we see that clearly in the churchocentric model.

Some discipling movements have abused the principles of discipleship by trying to run others' lives. No trainee should be required to get permission to miss church, make major household purchases, date, marry, leave town for vacation, and so on. Though accountability is vital to discipling, the autocratic approach such actions describe is a misapplication of the Christocentric model, and it was never intended to exist in the community of Christ.

The discipling church *is* a community of disciples and their leaders seeking to know God and do His will. Only when they are connected by a common core data and utilize His guidance tools, which are the apex of "remaining in Me," can this community disciple effectively.

3. In Training: Moving From Christ's Preparing Leaders Alone to a Leadership Community Engaged in Multilevel Training. The discipling church's training begins the first time a member of the discipling church makes contact with a person. Making disciples begins with introducing men and women to Christ. That statement alone smashes the traditional discipling parameters. Remember the definition of discipling we started with? "The intentional training of Christians, with accountability, on the basis of loving relationships." This is much broader than small groups or one-on-one encounters.

Broadening the discipling model is not a new idea, but the way it has been practiced by many churches is still too narrow for the church. Like the geneticist who reproduces the same DNA over and over outside the normal reproductive method, many churches have sought to create spiritual clones.

Traditionally, the discipling movement has attracted a certain kind of person: a verbally skilled, communication-oriented individual who sees a vision and goes for it. Such principle- and value-driven people love to make a difference and want a challenge. There is nothing wrong with being this way and liking these things, but problems arise when we start projecting our gifts and personality traits on others as a matter of spirituality. People like this—and I am one of them—tend to attract similar people and consider other types as unspiritual or apathetic.

I base my statement that the idea of broadening the discipling community is not new on Ephesians 4:11–16:[1]

It was he who gave some to be apostles, some to be prophets, some to be evangelists, and some to be pastors and teachers, to prepare God's people for works of service, so that the body of Christ may be built up until we all reach unity in the faith and in the knowledge of the Son of God and become mature, attaining to the whole measure of the fullness of Christ. Then we will no longer be infants, tossed back and forth by the waves, and blown here and there by every wind of teaching and by the cunning and craftiness of men in their deceitful scheming. Instead,

> speaking the truth in love, we will in all things grow
> up into him who is the Head, that is, Christ. From him
> the whole body, joined and held together by every
> supporting ligament, grows and builds itself up in
> love, as each part does its work.

This passage shows that the leadership of the local church should prepare people to be effective ministers for Jesus Christ. That includes helping them grow into spiritual maturity, and the end result is full employment of God's gifts through His people. When every member is doing his or her own part, the church will build itself up in love.

To get this job done, training or development must be multileveled. The word translated "prepare" in Ephesians 4:12 means "to train an athlete, to mend a broken bone, to restore something in disrepair." The work means more than training the spiritually well in ministry skills. Any church includes people in various stages of their walk with God: Some are in crisis; others are defeated; some are ready to be trained or ready to lead.

The discipling church is at least three things: a hospital for the spiritually sick, a greenhouse for the growth of new believers, and a training center for the eager and well.

Because the pastoral task is multidimensional and multileveled, the disciple-making pastor's task is to manage various levels of people development. Church leadership should be engaged in three primary areas of discipling.

The preaching/teaching track. Preaching is the first and most important step in the discipling process for the local church. However, I have been surprised at the number of people who consider discipling philosophy as the enemy of good preaching. Led by misconceptions, many have decided you can't be both a preaching pastor and a discipling pastor.

Without preaching, a disciple-making pastor is without his greatest tool. The pulpit ministry sets the church agenda, inspires, motivates, and paves the way for application vehicles.

"Come and see," "Come and follow Me," "Come and be with Me," and "Remain in Me" are all discipling. As soon as a person walks in the door and listens to a sermon he is taking an active part in it. Though he might only attend church and play on the softball team, discipling occurs. He is in the "Come and see" stage. The goal is to get him to take the next step and attach himself to a small group or some other part of the work. If that happens, he will have made the transition to "Come and follow Me." If he is leadership material and he takes specialized training, he will have entered "Come and be with Me."

The leadership track. Most churches lose their strength and die when they cease to produce new leaders. For training to really catch on in the discipling church, a community of loyalists—zealots, if you will—must be produced. A core of gifted learners willing to apprentice discipling philosophy and activity must be formed. They join the leadership community and reproduce themselves by developing their own apprentices each year.

Development of an ever-increasing leadership community insures the church's future. Even though a pastor claims to disciple by the preaching track, if he fails to form a leadership group, he has copped out. In order to widely implement and communicate discipling to the church populace, he must also develop leaders. Without this, reproduction does not exist, and multiplication cannot occur.

In the discipling church, the pastor and leadership team glean the leadership gifted from the congregation and place them in an environment that apprentices them so they may become reproducers and multipliers.

The small-group track. If churchocentric discipling provides multilevel training, it must be applied to the church through small-group ministry. Jesus modeled this when He exposed groups of people to the truth, followed by an invitation; He worked with those who responded. Today the small group still provides the church with the best vehicle for people development.

Once preaching has motivated people to go on with Christ, they need a vehicle into which they can channel their desire. When the invitations "Come and see" and "Come and follow Me" have been extended, the church channels that desire to say yes into small-group membership. It starts with a strong support emphasis, but the small group slowly graduates to more Bible and task emphasis (*see* Chart 3).

The group can continue to move along that path because the small-group leader guides it. He and his apprentice or assistant leader are members of the leadership community, which meets with the pastor and other church leaders. This small-group network cares for the needs of the church populace, identifies leaders for the leadership community, and fulfills the training and ministry skills Christians so vitally need.

4. In Outreach: Moving From Individual Evangelism to Evangelistic Teamwork. We see Christocentric evangelism in Jesus encountering Nicodemus, the woman at the well, and the rich young ruler. The modern parachurch has carried it on by training members to verbalize their faith as often as possible.

I believe every Christian has been charged with the responsibility to witness (2 Corinthians 5:18–20). Therefore I believe every Christian should be trained how to verbalize the Gospel (1 Peter 3:15). But I do not believe that most trained Christians will verbalize their faith in most situations. Why? For them to do so would violate their gift mix and compromise their ability to reach others for Christ.

That is a weird thing to say, isn't it? How could a person sabotage his ability to reach a person for Christ by verbalizing his faith? Let me explain. God has gifted each body member with a tool that is to be used in His kingdom's service (1 Peter 4:10). Some of these tools are to be employed in a supporting role in the community of faith; others are manifested on the front lines in communicating and teaching the faith. A per-

Chart 3
Small-Group Life

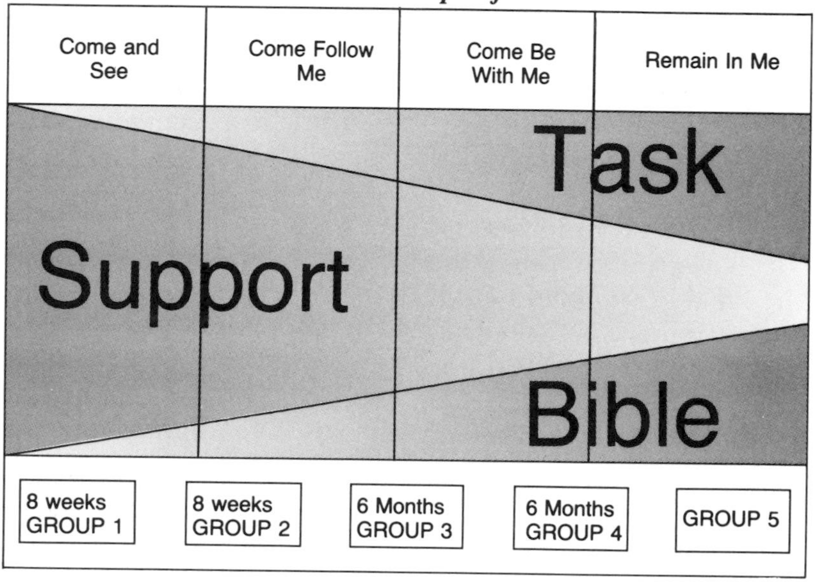

Come and See	Come Follow Me	Come Be With Me	Remain In Me

Task

Support

Bible

8 weeks GROUP 1	8 weeks GROUP 2	6 Months GROUP 3	6 Months GROUP 4	GROUP 5

Adapted From Lyman Coleman's *Serendipity Small Group Training*. For more resource information, contact Serendipity, P.O. Box 1012, Littleton, CO 80160.

son gifted at reaching others on a relational basis, by helping them through times of crisis, can hurt the process by verbalizing faith too quickly.

Yes, verbalization *should* take place, but when? The Christocentric model is aggressive, personal, and verbal. People with such gifts must be part of the churchocentric model, because no one can come to Christ without hearing the Gospel. But Jesus Himself explained an even more powerful way for the church to witness:

> "A new command I give you: Love one another. As I have loved you, so you must love one another. By this all men will know that you are my disciples if you love one another."
>
> John 13:34, 35

> . . . They broke bread in their homes and ate together with glad and sincere hearts, praising God and enjoying the favor of all the people. And the Lord added to their number daily those who were being saved.
>
> Acts 2:46, 47

In the churchocentric model, the key word is *shared.* Leadership, authority, God's guidance, and the training of the people are all shared. Now we learn evangelism is shared. The corporate witness of the church's love one for another creates a power and attraction that make verbalization a natural result. What greater power could there be than the love Jesus promised would make all people know we are His disciples?

We see this worked out in the first church, where loving commitment added to their number daily. How would you like to belong to a church that experienced such a wonderful harvest?

Functionally, how can outreach be a part of the discipling church?

Penetrate the world naturally. The verbalizers among us will always feel comfortable going for the gold every time. This type of person is needed in the church, and if the church faithfully discipled people, there would be more of them. But no matter how many verbalizers a church has, they will always be outnumbered by those who are not as verbal.

Usually verbalizers are teachers, and they tend to teach what works for them. This is why the aggressive verbalization mentality dominates the church. But even if every Christian consistently verbalized his faith, we would be less effective than we are when people play their proper body roles. For the church only to proclaim the Gospel would be like a boxer with only one arm. No matter how great your left hook, if you don't also have a right cross, you won't win many fights. The church needs the effective combination of love with feet on it and a strategically placed verbalization.

God has placed body members strategically in the world's harvest field. The church's challenge is to transform them from field residents to laborers. We can do this by communicating a more holistic evangelism approach. People need to be challenged to employ the gift of helps to minister to those in need and then network with the verbalizers in the congregation. For example, say I want to reach my work associate who has an interest in evolution and creation science. If I am a visually oriented person who reads a book about every decade, I can't talk about such matters with him. I may have taken him to a ball game or two and watered his lawn while he was on vacation, so he trusts me, but I cannot meet his need on this subject. Therefore I must introduce him to a differently gifted person who can meet that need. The disciple-making church helps me do that.

Artificial training does not translate into normal networks. So much of evangelism training does not focus on the use of spiritual gifts and natural networks, but on artificial means, like taking evangelistic teams to malls, to speak with strangers, or knocking on doors of people they do not know. Even church visitation is not a natural way of meeting people.

The problem is that even good training done in artificial

networks does not translate into normal life. In many cases the training goes to waste because Christians have been trained to speak directly to strangers or make a specific presentation. Those tactics don't work well with the people with whom we live, work, and play.

To reach the world, the church must become a team— one that coordinates its gifts and resources to reach the world. That requires the Holy Spirit's creativity, working through discipled members, the softness of the love gifts, the correctness of the word gifts, and the determination of the leadership gifts. Working together is the key.

5. In Pastoral Care: Moving From Christ Meeting All Needs Alone to Christ Meeting Needs Through Gifts of the Body.

What does good pastoral care have to do with discipleship, and what is its relationship to training? Without good pastoral care, you can't be a discipling church. Jesus is the good shepherd, the chief shepherd, who could and can meet every need. While He was on earth the disciples didn't have to look beyond Him, to any human, for their needs. As we have seen, the Christocentric discipling model places heavy emphasis on one person pouring his life into another.

In the churchocentric model, what Jesus was to the disciples, now the body members are to one another. That does not imply that body members are supernatural, but Christ chose to meet many body needs through other parts of the body. For example, I may pray to Christ for encouragement, and a friend may call me on the phone and pray with me. If I am sick, two Bible-study members may bring me a hot meal. Through His Spirit, God prompts members to minister to one another.

Decentralizing pastoral care. Historically pastoral care has been assigned to the clergy, when by rights it belongs to the entire church. Within the call to decentralization of ministry lies the decentralization of pastoral care. Many emotional-anchor types and people gifted in showing mercy, helps, giving, and exhortation or encouragement may be developed within the church as effective ministers.

Ephesians 4:16 points out that the church reaches its apex when each member is doing his part. As the discipling church decentralizes pastoral ministry, giving members permission to minister, they may actually do it better than the clergy.

> All the believers were one in heart and mind. No one claimed that any of his possessions was his own, but they shared everything they had. With great power the apostles continued to testify to the resurrection of the Lord Jesus and much grace was upon them all. There were no needy persons among them. . . .
>
> Acts 4:32–34

These verses show the obvious benefit of decentralization in the early church. Because the needs of the people had been met, powerful ministry became possible.

Pastoral care is discipling. Such a statement might seem shocking, but I am not claiming that pastoral care is all there is to discipling, any more than focusing on training in ministry skills or evangelism alone fills that bill. But when we place leadership development, training, and outreach together with pastoral care, we have discipling.

Pastoral care provides a foundation of life in the community of Christ that makes training and outreach possible (1 Thessalonians 2:7–12). Uncared-for people tend to become antagonistic and project their hurts on leadership. As a result, an adversarial relationship develops between church leaders and the congregation. On the other hand, when leaders create a loving and accepting environment, people can willingly drop many minor points of difference and work together.

Pastoral care is part of developing people toward maturity in Christ, so we must consider it discipling. People have special windows of opportunity in their lives when they are more open to God than normal. During those transitional or crisis periods, if the community of Christ is there, people will open themselves to Him. When people feel loved, they will drop their defenses and allow God's Word and people into their lives.

Pastoral training. Even if you desire to have decentralized pastoral care in the church, it will not happen without training. This will require several steps:

1. The people must know they are ministers and that they have contributions to make. Until they feel this confidence, they will not be able to act.
2. Christians need to discover and develop their specific gifts.
3. They need permission to experiment with their gifts in their area of interest.
4. Again and again they need to have this permission reinforced. In the face of failure they will need permission to try again, on a new track, to discover what went wrong and how it can be corrected. In success they need permission to try new things.
5. Pastorally gifted members need to recruit others to recruit and apprentice others, in order to multiply their efforts.

With this five-pronged program, a church can provide discipling that works within the congregation and reaches out to the world with the Gospel. As a result, people are better cared for, and body members find fulfillment in exercising their gifts.

Our model for the discipling process is based on the experiences of the early church. How did they develop such a multilevel discipling program? Let's take a look at how discipleship got started in the first church, at Jerusalem.

Part II

THE FIRST
CHURCH—JERUSALEM

The disciple-making church began to spread in Jerusalem. With the descent of the Holy Spirit, at Pentecost, the fledgling organization began to grow at a rate that almost defies imagination. All of it happened because the apostles followed the lessons they had learned from Jesus and led a small band to obey the Lord's command to preach the Gospel.

Along the way the apostles faced many problems and challenges that forced them to practice the methods and principles they had studied under Jesus for three years. Their response to that testing created a model of church growth that outlines the development of the church community from its first steps to full maturity. In the pages of the book of Acts we see the first fumbling steps of new converts and the failures they encountered. But we also see the message and principles they successfully spread to the entire world.

Ours are the problems and mistakes of the first church. So little has changed within congregations—and we have so much to learn.

3
Founding the First Church

Once Jesus ascended, the changes in Jerusalem's first church began. In the pages of Acts 2–7 we see the church's founding, over the course of about six years. Once the groundwork had been laid, evangelism started up under Philip, Stephen, and Peter; Acts 8–11 describes this growth, which occurred over two years.

Looking at the first five to seven years of the church, we can draw out its nature and characteristics. In some ways it parallels today's congregations. For example the Jerusalem church had a constitution, by-laws, a book of worship or church order, a doctrinal statement, even a purpose statement and an eight-year plan. Unlike congregations of today, none of this was written down by a committee; all such policies resided in the mental files of regenerate fishermen.

In principle, the church in Jerusalem had the same functions, the same Christ-commanded priorities, and the same internal conflicts as today's churches. In this section we'll take note of the special way the disciples processed and applied Christ's teachings to their congregations.

THE STAGES OF CHURCH DEVELOPMENT

As a church grows, it changes. Within the pages of the New Testament, we see how the early church altered and developed. We may apply these patterns to our churches.

The three churches of the New Testament (*the first church, mission church,* and *discipling church*) went through four broad stages. As we primarily focus on Paul's methods, men, travels, and writings, we will see these phases in the forty-year apostolic ministry:

FORMATIVE PHASE: All definitions of *formative* have as their basis the idea of structuring or shaping something. Likewise, in this stage of the church the apostles provided structure, creating a new, growing entity. They began with preaching that resulted in conversions and by grouping new believers into manageable units for development.

DEVELOPMENTAL PHASE: Once they had laid founda-tions, the apostles had to develop principles around which they could build local church life. They created corporate structure, standardized practices, and estab-lished a way of life. Within Scripture, overarching de-scriptions and cameos describe this process.

CORRECTIVE PHASE: In the developed church, the leaders had to adjust imbalances and address abuses and rebellions against priorities and practices. Some churches find this stage becomes a way of life.

Within this phase, we can also include more positive correction measures that come with obedience and the roles internal and external opposition play in maturation.

REPRODUCTIVE PHASE: Unlike Jerusalem, many churches never reach this stage. Until the church reproduces both on a widespread individual basis and at the corporate level, the church remains incomplete. A local congregation must effectively evangelize its harvest field and reproduce by church planting.

I provide these phases as communication tools, places where we can hang the facts and learn to apply them. It will help if we understand that all four work simultaneously throughout a church.

Why Are the Phases Important?

With these phases, I hope to help you see the progressive nature of church maturation. Focus on your present ministry: Are you stalled out in one phase? You may break out of it.

The journey from the first church at Jerusalem to the discipling church at Ephesus took twenty years. During that time a great deal of processing took place in the mind of Paul and in the churches' practice. Much of it was hammered out in debate and on the anvil of human experiences.

The church's priorities did not change during that time, but its practices evolved. Within the first church, mission church, and discipling church, we see the principles Jesus taught and practiced. Though the scriptural literature is limited, as Peter so eloquently writes, we have all we need (2 Peter 1:3).

JERUSALEM'S FORMATIVE STAGE

Like a soldier's initial reaction to gunfire or a mother's response to her baby's cry, the disciples' first inclination reveals a great deal. The twelve, along with the others in the Upper Room, didn't have time to write a strategy. Before they could analyze their experience, they were running down the streets, preaching the Gospel in tongues they hadn't learned. Bouncing about in their heads were memories of how to do things, which Jesus had said the Helper would restore to them, in a workable order: "But the Counselor, the

Chart 4
The First Church

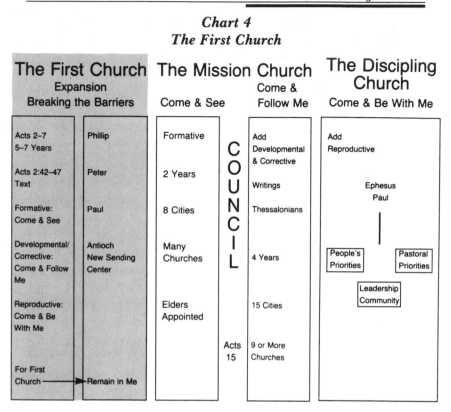

The First Church
Expansion
Breaking the Barriers

The Mission Church
Come & See   Come &
                    Follow Me

The Discipling Church
Come & Be With Me

Acts 2–7 5–7 Years	Phillip	Formative		Add Developmental & Corrective	Add Reproductive
Acts 2:42–47 Text	Peter	2 Years	C O U N C I L	Writings	
Formative: Come & See	Paul	8 Cities		Thessalonians	Ephesus Paul
Developmental/ Corrective: Come & Follow Me	Antioch New Sending Center	Many Churches		4 Years	
Reproductive: Come & Be With Me		Elders Appointed		15 Cities	
			Acts 15	9 or More Churches	
For First Church ──▶	Remain in Me				

People's Priorities   Pastoral Priorities

Leadership Community

Holy Spirit, whom the Father will send in my name, will teach you all things and *will remind you of everything* I have said to you" (John 14:26, *italics added*).

The apostles knew they would witness, but how would they get out of Jerusalem, to Judea, Samaria, and finally to the farthest reaches of the world? Their visceral reaction to both supernatural and natural events arose from their organized memories of Jesus. That reaction reveals their deeply held and practiced beliefs.

Launching the Jerusalem Church

Like a purposeful ballistic missile, the Jerusalem church burst with extraordinary power upon the city. As 120 wide-eyed men and women stumbled into the streets, babbling jabberwocky, it appeared to be the climax of a drunken orgy. But ten days of prayer, a filled spirit, and over three years of training made Peter's response to the situation possible.

The amazed crowds thought the babblers had gone off their rockers. However, when Peter stood and spoke, no one expressed surprise; Peter knew what to do with a crowd. Once his Teacher had stood in a mass of worshipers, just as the priest was pouring water over the altar, symbolizing God's promise of the coming of the Spirit, and He said, "If any man is thirsty, let him come to me and drink. . . . From his innermost being will flow rivers of living water" (*see* John 7:37, 38 NAS). During the feast of Passover, Peter's Teacher called Himself the bread of life. Jesus had taken advantage of every situation, and Peter began to live out that lesson.

The promised Spirit had filled Peter's heart, and the words of the prophet Joel came to mind (Joel 2:28–32). Peter explained Pentecost, exalted Christ, and exhorted his listeners to commitment. He contextualized his message to the Jewish audience that believed the Old Testament.

The Message Declared. Inherent in this story we see principles for starting a church. Inspired people communicate a message to those captured by a demonstration of the power of God. The message came from a respected and authoritative source, and hearers were called to a decision and action.

> When the people heard this, they were cut to the heart and said to Peter and the other apostles, "Brothers, what shall we do?" Peter replied, "Repent and be baptized, every one of you, in the name of Jesus Christ for the forgiveness of your sins. And you will receive the gift of the Holy Spirit. The promise is for you and your children and for all who are far off—for all whom the Lord our God will call."
>
> Acts 2:37–39

When people respond to the Gospel, they need a call to action they can understand. The Jews understood repentance, both from their history and the ministry of John the Baptist. Culturally it was the line of demarcation that indicated they were serious.

From Jesus, Peter had learned to explain eternal life in a contextualized way. To the woman at the well, Jesus was living water; Nicodemus He called to be born again; the rich young ruler He told to sell all he had; and Zacchaeus had to pay back all the money he had stolen. The action each took depended on the point of conflict, the exact area that tested commitment. With thousands before him, Peter gave a relevant but general means of sealing their commitment to Christ.

THE MODERN FORMATIVE STAGE

Today's church start-ups must possess the characteristics of the Jerusalem church. Inspired people must still communicate a contextualized message to those who have been gathered by creative, powerful means. Whether it be signs and wonders, as in Jerusalem, or telemarketing, attention getters are vital.

Church planters must be well taught and trained in the six-step method employed by Christ:

1. Tell them what.
2. Tell them why.
3. Show them how.
4. Do it with them.
5. Let them do it.
6. Deploy them.[1]

A combination of on-the-job training and cognitive material creates leaders of unusual conviction. Based on experience, trained leaders will have the "spiritual savvy" to transform most situations into teaching laboratories. They will apply their principled convictions to needs.

I teach that discipling begins the moment someone walks in the door of the church. The environment itself begins the process of interesting someone in knowing Jesus Christ. The initial stage of discipling, "Come and see," is a gathering phase in which the church motivates, inspires, and exhorts people toward more serious commitment to Christ. Beginning with evangelism, Christians tell the story, so a person can make a decision. In the first church Peter began the discipling process and immediately had 3,000 convert-disciples.

Never fall for the canard that discipling only means training in skill and accumulation of knowledge or that it should be a department of the church. Disciple making involves everything, from preevangelism to leadership development. For that reason, church-centered discipling works best. In such a system, the entire environment and gifts of the church can network to produce the most balanced and best-trained Christians.

During the formative stage, the church gathers people who are recipients of a hopeful message, given by inspired communicators. Next, prepared communicators guide newly converted disciples into growth. All four stages of church development have distinctive markings, yet they take place at the same time, too, resulting in overlap. In the first church the formative and developmental worked in concert.

The 3,000 converts flowed into a corporate culture designed by the well-taught, deeply rooted convictions of the apostles. Though Acts 2:42–47 gives the impression that all this took place at once, I suspect a reasonable time lapse occurred, during which the apostles organized the church and developed believers. The process beginning in Acts 2:42 and ending in Acts 2:47 requires years to develop.

4
Practices and Priorities
of the First Church

Many Christians tend to glamorize the first church, ignoring certain realities. Modern churchmen frustrated with local-church administration often lament, "Oh, how I wish I could have been part of that first church. They didn't have to sit through business meetings, wrestle with problem people, and deal with endless administrative detail." They could hardly have a more mythological view of that church. In fact the early church had all the difficulties and responsibilities of the modern church—and more.

If we learn anything from the apostles' early behavior, we know they called a meeting immediately following the great harvest of 3,000 souls. In the Upper Room they chose Judas's replacement (Acts 1). When faced with internal problems concerning food distribution, they again dealt with it by meeting (Acts 6). Whether the subject under discussion was whether or not to accept Gentiles into the church (Acts 11), what Gentiles were required to do (Acts 15), or Paul's formal submission of the Gospel to their authority (Galatians 1), the apostles were deliberate men who did not shrink from administrative meetings.

The majority of the converts stayed in Jerusalem. Although many were pilgrims, the supernatural serendipity they had experienced compelled them to remain. Supposing only a third of the converts had been non-Jerusalem residents, placing 1,000 people in Christian homes would have been a nightmare. These people didn't just naturally make their way there. By necessity a coordinated effort must have been made by—guess who? Before the apostles could go house to house, ministering to the variety of needs, they had to have a systematic way to get a handle on these people.

Surely some of the apostles had the gift of administration. Just because the descriptions of highlights of the Jerusalem church do not provide administrative details, that does not mean the apostles did not have to labor through long, sometimes boring meetings. An earmark of early church formation and development is good stewardship of the fruit God has given.

EARLY CHURCH PRACTICES AND PRIORITIES

In the six- or seven-year period covered in Acts 2–7, some verses focus on a specific occurrence, while other texts describe the church's corporate culture in terms of priorities and practices. Peter's sermon (Acts 2:14–40), for example, is a specific event that took ten minutes. The priorities and practices described in Acts 2:42–47 characterize the principles of church life as it took place over the course of several years. In fact, these principles probably continued throughout the life of the Jerusalem church.

In these priorities and practices, Jesus' discipling principles are foundational. Well taught, the early disciples made disciple making their top priority. Discipling principles were second nature in everything they did.

Acts 2:42 begins, "They devoted themselves to the apostles' teaching. . . ." What had the apostles taught? I don't think their lessons differed from the pattern Paul exhorted his followers to obey: "What you heard from me, keep as the pattern of sound teaching . . ." (2 Timothy 1:13). Galatians 2:6–10 makes it clear the apostles had checked out Paul's message; the apostles' teaching and Paul's Gospel agreed. The Gospel means more than the bare facts of salvation. The Good News includes all revelation: the grand sweep of Romans, Galatians, and Ephesians, the specific corrective teachings of Corinthians and Colossians, the needs met in Philippians and the Thessalonian letters. The whole counsel of God is the Gospel. Three times Paul called the pattern of teaching or sound doctrine a deposit (2 Timothy 1:14; 2:2; 4:2–4); the Gospel is a sacred deposit God has entrusted to faithful workers.

Speaking to the Corinthians about Timothy, Paul tells us a great deal about the standardization of the Gospel message: ". . . He will remind you of my way of life in Christ Jesus, which agrees with what I teach everywhere in every church" (1 Corinthians 4:17). What Paul learned, he passed on intact.

Putting Discipling at the Heart of the Church

The apostles' teachings started with the person of Christ, humanity's need for Him, and the importance of spreading this message to the entire world. They provided a system of teaching—a doctrinal statement, if you will—and the people devoted themselves to it. The syntax of Acts 2:42–47 gives a sense of what is needed for effective formation and development of community. It does so by the extensive use of the imperfect tense:

"Devoted themselves" (v. 42).
"Was filled" (v. 43).
"Were together" (v. 44).
"Selling" (v. 45).
"Continued" (v. 46).
"[Kept] praising, enjoying favor" (v. 47).

In all, the five verses use the imperfect eight times. This tense indicates a continuous behavior that can best be depicted by a person who enters a theater when a film is in progress. The film is showing when he enters and when he leaves. Regardless of what time he enters, leaves, and reenters, or the number of times he goes in and out, the film is still showing.

In the Jerusalem church, the apostles' priorities and practices—to which Christians intensely devoted themselves—became a way of life. True spiritual formation requires such commitment to consistency of practice. The actions of the first church confirm discipling was at its heart, and if we had nothing but this text to show us the way, it would be enough to make our churches discipling centers.

Five priorities practiced by the Jerusalem church developed it into a mature, reproductive congregation:

1. A commitment to Scripture (Acts 2:42).
2. A commitment to one another (Acts 2:42, 44, 46).
3. A commitment to prayer (Acts 2:42).
4. A commitment to praise and worship (Acts 2:43, 47).
5. A commitment to outreach (Acts 2:45–47).

Commitment to Scripture. The apostles began to teach the great truths about Jesus Christ by showing their distinctively Jewish congregation how the Old Testament prophets showed He was Messiah. They taught Jesus' teachings on life, death, and the eternal state.

In a culture hostile to the Christian "heresy," the apostles had to follow this up with practical application. The teaching Christ had modeled for them meant more than talking. He had told them what should be done and why; then He had allowed them to practice the behavior themselves. Once He thought they understood, He deployed them to put that learning into action.

Jesus had demonstrated that the Word was the basis of belief, and the apostles passed on that priority. This centrality of the written Word is self-evident in their teaching. They make clear that supernatural dimensions interface with God's Word (1 Thessalonians 2:13; 2 Timothy 3:16, 17; Hebrews 4:12; 1 Peter 2:3, 4). In order to have a healthy formation or spiritual development, all believers need the nourishment and training of Scripture.

Scripture transforms the mind of the Christian (Romans 12:2). People may change the way they think and react for a number of reasons—external events, emotional experiences, or cognitive principles may influence them—but all such changes must be routed through the mind. That is why it is so important for Christians to have a working knowledge of Scripture. They should memorize and meditate on it and be able to defend and explain their faith from it.

Today's evangelical church has come to its anemic state primarily because of widespread ignorance of scriptural truth. Uninformed Christians do not have a well-programmed grid from which to make good choices. Their data bases, programmed with bad information, have no organized places in which to process and store information.

The solution begins with an intense devotion to scriptural truth and church-provided vehicles that assist in application. Biblical knowledge alone has no power; but energized by a joint effort of an activated human and the Holy Spirit, biblical knowledge becomes a mighty weapon.

A Commitment to One Another. "They devoted themselves . . . to the fellowship . . ." (Acts 2:42). The word for "fellowship" is *koinonia,* meaning "to have in common." What does this mean? The text serves as its own commentary when it says, "All the believers were together . . ." (2:44). In light of physical circumstances, such togetherness was necessary. The actual housing of thousands of visitors required those with newfound faith to huddle together.

In the latter part of the twentieth century, the importance of all believers being together remains, but for a different reason. Believers cannot share life together unless they *are* together on a regular basis. In a mobile, rootless, "cut flower" society such as ours, Christian contact becomes critical.

". . . Continuing with one mind" (2:46 NAS) indicates the Jerusalem Christians understood their objective and knew they were together for more than simple physical contact. Yes, their togetherness provided security, but continual trips to the temple indicate both a commitment to evangelize and a desire not to break too quickly from their cultural roots. Members of this new thing called the church shared *everything,* including spiritual oneness. Like children on the first day of school, together they experienced excitement, fear, and a passion to know everything. In the face of persecution, a common goal held them together as a church.

One of the oversights of modern discipling teachers is a lack of appreciation for the necessity of community in holistic spiritual development. Communitylessness seriously handicaps the rich variety offered in the local church. Many discipling leaders would readily agree with this, but would quickly protest that community only works in a healthy church. I agree. One of the ironies of the church is that a healthy one becomes the most powerful and dynamic force for good on the planet; on the other hand, a sick church is one of the ugliest sights known to man.

The first church had strikingly simple priorities and practices. Twice this passage in Acts 2 mentions the breaking of bread. The Christians ate, sang, played, and prayed together. Often they followed a regular meal with communion celebration. They shared more than superficial fellowship— digging deep in powerful *koinonia,* which meant more than money, material goods, and prized possessions. "All the believers were together and had everything in common. Selling their possessions and goods, they gave to anyone as he had need" (2:44, 45).

This fellowship was without question new. Before Pentecost, the disciples' attitude had reflected anything but altruism. "Who will be the greatest?" they had asked. "Who will get the celestial box seats next to the Lord?" God's new invention, started by the Holy Spirit, brought radical change. Christian commitment to one another was genuine in Jerusalem, and the birth of this new community forever changed the way the apostles and their followers related to one another and the world around them.

Let's not forget that in its formative stage the first church had no organism like itself to follow. The apostles blazed a new trail, basing decisions on their training. Since Jesus had told them a disciple would be like his teacher, they modeled their work after Him. What else could they have done? What else would God expect of them?

Some people question that Jesus had a strategy or that the Gospel writers present one in their description of His ministry. The greatest apologetic for Christ's strategy is the disciples' behavior. Their actions reveal His strategy.

When Christ ascended and invented the church, the disciple-making model didn't become less vital or take a backseat to any other priorities—it changed. Making disciples remained fresh in the apostles' minds. They began with evangelism, and in one day they had 3,000 new converts on their hands. Soon they had 5,000 and then 10,000. Christ had prepared them for this, but they had never expected such results. When Jesus had said they would do greater things than He, I suspect they didn't really believe it.

Commitment to community meant commitment to one another. The logistical nightmare required a relational miracle. When people started sharing everything, particularly material goods, they realized Jesus had worked that miracle.

During the five- to seven-year time frame Acts 2:42–47 describes, the Jerusalem church moved from the formative stage into the developmental one. Naturally it shifted from the Christocentric to the churchocentric model. The ascension of Christ, the arrival of the Spirit, and the giving of spiritual gifts all called for the switch.

Community made discipling possible by creating a warm environment. When people feel accepted or safe, they drop their defenses, set aside excuses, and begin to move spiritually. The Jerusalem Christians had gotten beyond coffee and doughnuts; their conversation had bridged the treacherous chasm between the world, the weather, and work and cares, conflicts, and concerns. Because they spent large volumes of time together, eating, working, and playing together, they could make this crucial transition.

The body of Christ needs to have enough fun together to set the stage for accountability and obedience. When a parent takes time to have fun with a child, he builds up relational equity that makes it much easier for the child to obey when friction occurs. The bond causes the child to say, "Okay, I'll do it for you, even though I disagree."

In the body of Christ, living and playing together smooth the way for moments when people must go along with the tougher tasks required of the church. The first church's community made survival possible in the face of imminent rigors. This dynamic, magnetic church not only experienced the positives, they also shared the privilege of the fellowship of suffering. While the modern church tends to think of itself as having it all, in reality it is extremely poor in many ways. The wealth of the Jerusalem community is not often ours!

A Commitment to Prayer. A man was overheard defining *status quo* as, "That's Latin for 'the mess we're in.' " Prayer attacks the status quo, striking at the root of issues, moving God's hand, and catapulting angels into action.

If you believe the above, you will pray.

The first church committed itself to prayer, and I can make that assertion because the Bible uses the imperfect tense to describe their praying. I've heard it said that the first church prayed ten days, preached ten minutes, and saw 3,000 come to Christ. The modern church prays ten minutes, preaches ten days, and sees a handful come to Christ. Prayer is not a corporate priority now as it was in the church's early days.

The first church prayed in the Upper Room, in the temple, and in their homes. They prayed in anticipation, in thanksgiving, and in crisis; and they prayed for needs.

Several examples demonstrate the first church's prayer portfolio. First and most impressive, we see the ten days in the Upper Room, when the disciples waited for something to happen. Acts 2:42–47 indicates that throughout the stages of its development, prayer was woven into the normal, corporate church day.

The first prayer in crisis, recorded in Acts 4, reveals a great deal about the strength of the apostles' teaching and the community. When the church heard of Peter and John's release by the Sanhedrin, their prayers show a worldview concerning difficulty and opposition that is the direct antithesis of the contemporary church's. Their prayers are filled with gratitude, even wonder, that God considered them worthy of suffering. The *koinonia* of suffering did much to build conviction and community—possibly even more than the text indicates.

The ongoing process of growth described in Acts 2:42–47 is proactive and essential, but alone it takes too long and remains incomplete. The reactive fellowship of suffering reveals the church's character. To balance the church, God joins the proactive and reactive. In fact, a church that does not know hardship is untested. Until it faces trials and proves itself, it remains an incomplete community.

When the believers first raised their voices to God, they thanked Him that He was in control. They quoted Psalm 2, which proclaims God's sovereign orchestration of all human events. Naming the present and powerful of their day—Herod, Pontius Pilate, and the officials of the religious establishment—the believers proclaimed these men helpless in the face of God. They ended with a call for God to stretch out His hand and take action—not to protect, but to do more miracles, signs, and wonders, so that others would know Christ.

God was pleased. He shook the place, and the Christians were renewed in the Spirit, and they left there to proclaim the Word with even greater boldness.

Jerusalem's believers saw difficulty as a sign of doing right; it encouraged them to press harder. They saw opposition as an indication of progress. Their praying revealed this spirit. Such a unique worldview was not originally theirs; they had learned it from their teachers, the apostles.

When well-taught believers confront a challenge, their character rises to the occasion, and they grow. The work improves, and the Gospel is preached more widely and with greater power. Positive response to resistance makes it possible for people to break through barriers. Like weight lifting, working through spiritual resistance makes one stronger—and to be stronger means to have greater capacity, to take on more than ever.

The apostles modeled the priority of prayer. In the multiple meetings from house to house and in the temple, they taught it, showing people how to do it. Their refusal to allow the conflict over the order of food distribution for widows to distract them from prayer (Acts 6:1–7) also communicated volumes.

A few years later, more results of this teaching would show up in the response the church had when Peter was thrown into a Jerusalem prison. The church prayed together, and he was released.

Jerusalem's church evidences the commitment to prayer. Acts allows us to peer through a few windows that give us a clear view of its prayer life. Like Jerusalem's congregation, a praying church acts as though God is alive and therefore considers it a priority to take time to talk to Him.

E. M. Bounds wrote: "The men who have most fully illustrated Christ in their character, and have most powerfully affected the world for Him, have been men who have spent so much time with God as to make it a notable feature in their lives."[1] The first church was much for God, because they spent much time with God.

A Commitment to Praise or Worship. A church's commitment to praise—or as some call it, worship—provides a most telling indicator of its health. The commitment to praise God comes from the heart.

In the Jerusalem church, the devotion to the apostles'

teaching, to one another, and prayer combined to create an electric environment that demanded praise. "Everyone was filled with awe . . ." (Acts 2:43). "Awe" literally means "soul fear," a deep respect for God and what He was doing. ". . . They . . . ate together with glad and sincere hearts, praising God and enjoying the favor of all the people . . ." (Acts 2:46, 47). The proactive, ongoing process had moved the church through the formative stage, into the developmental one, and now the reproductive stage was beginning to emerge. Enthusiasm made ministry a natural overflow of internal experience. The "awe factor" describes the environmental change after Christ ascended.

When Christ left the church, He left the Helper, the Holy Spirit, who would reside in every believer. Each believer would be supernaturally joined together in the living organism called the church. Now the church would meet some of the needs Christ had previously met. Under His leadership, as the head, the body would minister to one another. Believers would find the care, relationships, and varieties of abilities required for a fully taught disciple within the community. Paul referred to this as preparing God's people for the work of service (Ephesians 4:12).

With the recent surge of interest in church planting has come an intense interest in creating environment. The lack of a praise environment, not a lack of technical know-how, most hinders the contemporary church.

Avant-garde church planters, those on the cutting edge, have begun to till new ground on environment—sadly, it is the wrong ground. They advocate psychographs and building the message around felt need. Demographics design the worship service, and they focus music and other characteristics around the congregation's likes and dislikes. Use drama, special effects, and whatever can be found that will hold the congregation's interest, these church planters advise. Make church fun and exciting.

I have nothing against any of the above, if leaders do them ethically and within the bounds of good taste. However, I do not believe the worship environment they seek can be found through such techniques. These merely simulate a real, Spirit-engendered environment, while their artificial nature highlights the talent and abilities of man. A spiritual buzz based on a highly gifted person's presentation will require a long string of buzzes. That, of course, leads to a desensitizing that eventually becomes boredom.

The Acts text says the first-church members "kept feeling a sense of awe." That ongoing awe was built on a Spirit-engendered environment that provided a constant stream of events, maintaining the excitement for the seven years described. The Jerusalem awe factor was a *10*—believers must have felt nearly giddy.

When signs, wonders, and miracles combine with teaching, prayer, and community, you get critical mass. You can't keep the lid on; something's got to give, and usually it manifests itself in a burst of praise. You might describe the first church as the original contagious congregation.

This kind of environment not only allowed ministry, it nourished it. That is why the apostles did so many miracles. The people were amazed and experienced wonder, which led to praise.

Luke further describes the atmospheric conditions: "gladness." No one manufactured this behavior; people had opened their homes because they desired it. They possessed sincerity of heart and no hidden agendas; they just liked spending time together, especially in worship. Real worship is the product of a healthy church, not of smoke and mirrors. The ongoing no-nonsense practice of commitments to the basic building blocks form the basis of this text.

"Worship is the purpose of the church!" people often tell me. This philosophy says, "The church's first priority is to praise God." By that they mean worship must be done verbally and come from the heart, via music and other vehicles of expression.

I agree the ultimate expression of our submission and

love for God is to fall down before Him and say thank You. The powerful images in John's Revelation portray such events. I desire to praise God and give Him the honor He deserves. However, I have a problem with presenting worship as the church's top priority.

What kind of person truly praises God? What would God rather see in His people—obedience or sacrifice? (1 Samuel 15:22). The Bible clearly says God chooses obedience, because it is the grandest form of worship (Romans 12:1, 2). Singing and praising God seem better in a setting dominated by Christian leaders and other mature Christians, because they praise God from the depths of their commitment and experience.

I contend that the church's purpose is to glorify God by making healthy, reproducing disciples. Therefore, the church reaches out to fulfill the commission. When obedient believers become fully engaged in His mandates, they worship God with more vigor than anyone.

Such an atmosphere is not manufactured but comes from a Spirit-engendered praise that delights God's heart. Worship does not train and develop people for ministry; it expresses the heart-felt awe of those trained and developed as disciples. Worship is the *result* of God's working in us, not the *cause*.

A Commitment to Outreach. Both praise and outreach result from the environment created by God's Spirit. When His people committedly practice digging into God's Word, praying together, and sharing their lives in community, worship will erupt. Just try to keep people from reaching out then!

Outreach goes in two directions: in the body, and outside the body.

In the Body. "Selling their possessions and goods, they gave to anyone as he had need" (Acts 2:45). The Jerusalem church's devotion went deep. How many modern believers sell property and give to the needy? How about the sports car, the boat, or the golf clubs? Such actions caught the world's attention then and would more so now. In our "get ahead, get as much as you can" world, the idea of selling valuable materials and donating them to others is rare enough to make the six o'clock news.

The only criterion for such giving was need. Jesus had told the founders of the first church, "A new commandment I give you, that you love one another, even as I have loved you, that you also love one another. By this all men will know that you are My disciples, if you have love for one another" (John 13:34, 35 NAS).

Outside the Body. Part of church outreach is what the church is before the watching world. People desire love, to be cared for and belong. When they see a loving, caring community, they feel a natural attraction. This type of caring cuts through cultural resistance like a knife through butter. Never underestimate the power of a mature, Christlike community ". . . enjoying the favor of all the people" (Acts 2:47). Before their irresistible and magnetic power, skeptics fall limp.

The lives of people like Mother Teresa and Dietrich Bonhoeffer display the visual communication power of Christ's love. By seeking nothing in return, they communicate sacrifice and interest in the weak and helpless.

Many have likened the Gospel to a song. Visual gospel displays represent the music. The verbalization of the message represents the words of the song. Truly effective outreach requires both words and song. Outside the backdrop of the caring church community, evangelism becomes outreach with one hand tied behind its back. Too often mission-oriented leaders and the local church have not gotten together on this, with debilitating results for both.

The first church put first things first, devoting themselves to practicing the priorities; therefore God rewarded them and increased the responsibility of those doing right. He considered them worthy of greater stewardship so He added to their number.

Later Paul would teach, "I planted, Apollos watered, but God was causing the growth" (1 Corinthians 3:6 NAS). If one seeks a biblical measuring stick for effective evangelism, it would be God's daily adding to the body those being saved (Acts 2:47).

The standard is high, but the battle is the Lord's. Obedient churches seek the ultimate goal of conversions on a regular basis. The first church employed various evangelistic methods: They met the public at the temple and went from house to house—a simple strategy that worked, because the average believer would talk about his newfound faith with his network. Regardless of the corporate church's outreach strategy, no substitute exists for the unspectacular daily witness of its members.

Sick churches don't have positive environments; therefore evangelism becomes a heavily cranked-up program—and a "gas hog." This system requires a great deal of energy and manipulation that would become unnecessary if the members' lives caught fire. Spiritual sterility—corporately or individually—is no virtue.

The first church grew because God counted the people worthy of the trust. It grew because there were many to reach. Because the people practiced God's priorities, as taught by the apostles, the community expanded.

The apostles had passed on to the first church the five commitments Jesus had taught them. If a contemporary church effectively practiced three of the five, it would be powerful; if it achieved four of the five, it would become a great church. Any pastor who wishes to know how to build a great church will find everything he needs to know in the first one.

5
Challenges for a Growing Church

One of my childhood joys involved taking a detached bike tire and pushing it, to see how far down the street it could travel before it veered off and hit something. Sometimes I watched it roll for over a city block, but I always knew that at some point the wheel would begin to wobble and turn and would end up bouncing off a car or something else. If I was lucky, before it fell, it would bounce high, thrilling my corrupted little mind.

A bike tire is not built to travel on its own. Unless it has a framework and a rider to guide it, it will lack direction and power. In the same way, the church cannot endlessly, steadily travel down one path—it requires a corrective stage.

THE CHURCH'S CORRECTIVE STAGE

When the church does well and everything hums along, leaders need to make midcourse corrections if they want that success to continue. As a church matures and addresses the human-frailty problems that make the church such a challenge, fine-tuning helps keep everything on course. On the other hand, if church efforts have negative results, correction becomes an immediate necessity.

We have seen how the first church moved through the formative and developmental stages. While these still took place, the congregation began to experience the corrective stage. In order to mature properly, the church needed new experiences and course alterations.

Persecution as Correction

In Acts 4 Luke tells us that Peter and John's preaching had landed them in the Jewish supreme court. The 3,000 had become 5,000. As a result of this unprecedented conversion growth, they got into trouble. (Some trouble—it's the kind Christ *wants* His church in!) Measured by the crème de la crème of measuring sticks—conversion growth—the church had great success.

Once converted, the Christians grew in understanding of the apostles' teaching. Faced with their leaders' troubles, they demonstrated increased cohesiveness and strength of character in their prayer (Acts 4:24–30). Every church can envy such prayers and set them as a goal. Peter and John's persecution facilitated growth in the lives of first-church members, because it resulted in that prayer.

When the apostles stood before the Jewish leaders, the leaders saw what had become evident to the church: "When they saw the courage of Peter and John and realized that they were unschooled, ordinary men, they were astonished and they took note that these men had been with Jesus" (Acts 4:13).

"We can't stop. You can kill us, but we won't stop." The apostles' response fueled the fire of the church community and put the religious establishment on notice that they confronted the genuine article. External opposition caused the church to take corrective action they would not have taken under ordinary conditions. Members of the congregation were called upon to pray and consider losing all their leaders, their own lives, and all forms of safety and security. The situation required that they fixate on the apostles' worldview. As a result, believers received a fresh endowment of God's Spirit and a bolstering of confidence (Acts 4:31).

Regenerate humankind naturally seeks to avoid conflict, to take the path of least resistance, and to desire comfort. The Christian finds such desires dashed on the rocks of obedience as he ventures into the opposing environment. As new Christians are produced, the best opposition also appears.

Repeatedly the first church experienced conflict with its powerful enemies in the religious establishment. Some believers were jailed; Steven and James lost their lives. Later, in the best example of corrective persecution, the first church scattered from Jerusalem, to preach the Gospel.

In His genius, God uses our effective obedience to create greater dependence and acts of faith that move us to maturity. Had they not taken place, our lives would have remained underdeveloped. So it was with the first church.

Internal Corrective Action

The church always becomes better after a corrective action. Numbers increase, disciples become more resolved in purpose, and the power of God and preaching have never been more effective. Immediately following the persecution and prayer described in Acts 4, the first church began a roll:

> All the believers were one in heart. . . . No one claimed that any of his possessions was his own, but they shared everything they had. . . . Much grace was upon them all. There were no needy. . . . From time to time those who owned lands or houses sold them, brought the money from the sales and put it at the apostles' feet. . . .
>
> Acts 4:32–35

But fallen man, even regenerate fallen man, has proven he cannot stand consistent spiritual prosperity. The flesh naturally corrupts a good thing. When people give, others take notice. The most natural thing is to thank a giving person, admire him, and give him extra attention. Equally commonly, others follow suit. Possibility for corruption also remains ever present. The first church's first internal conflict came hot on the heels of its ministry roll.

More than likely Ananias and his wife, Sapphira, were members in good standing at the first church. The well-intentioned couple simply cut a few ethical corners. (How many of us have not exaggerated our spiritual feats?) Wanting to be part of what God was doing in the electric environment of the first church, they sold their summer-home lot. They prayed about it, and it seemed hard to give up that dream. But they saw the needs in the body, and they could do something to get in on the action.

Ananias decided not to give all the money. There was nothing wrong with that; in fact, he did not *have* to give the money at all. Dishonesty came into the act when he represented to the leadership that he *had* given the full sale price.

Peter accused him simply: "Ananias, how is it that Satan has so filled your heart that you have lied to the Holy Spirit. . . ?" (Acts 5:3).

Many have puzzled over the unremitting severity of the death penalty for both Ananias and his wife. But example setting has its place, and this established a precedent at the first church: Dishonesty and all other forms of clearly obstinate sin would not be tolerated. God wanted to make a point of the preciousness of the environment that created such dynamic ministry.

Two telling comments by Luke prove the effectiveness of this corrective action:

> "Great fear seized the whole church and all who heard about these events" (Acts 5:11). The correction emotionally galvanized the church. At the inauguration of any project, leaders must immediately and firmly deal with cultural values. With the salvation of mankind at stake, the physical lives of two Christians seems a small sacrifice.

"The apostles performed many miraculous signs and wonders among the people. And all the believers used to meet together in Solomon's Colonnade. No one else dared join with them, even though they were highly regarded by the people. Nevertheless, more and more men and women believed in the Lord and were added to their number" (Acts 5:12–14). As a result of the correction, the Christians were thought of even more highly, and many came to faith in Christ.

Firm corrective action over internal problems yielded a healthy fear of sin and a greater fruit in ministry, something today's church has yet to learn.

The apostles had learned these methods from Jesus, who dealt directly with problems. He confronted the twelve about their priorities in Mark 10:35–45, their lack of faith in Mark 4, and their misunderstanding the cross in Mark 8:32–38. Naturally the apostles followed Him, confronting blatant dishonesty head-on.

Disobedient leadership avoids the tough corrective issues, because, *If we offend them, we lose money as well as all their friends and extended family.* Obedient leaders face criticism, slander, and everything else that goes with doing the right thing in a tough situation. It's not a question of whether or not leaders are willing to pay the price, because a price *will* be paid. Rather, they must ask, *Which price do we want to pay?*

Will church leaders face the misunderstanding, the emotional pressure, the loss of key families, and possibly the loss of a job? Or will they allow known "sin in the camp" to curse a ministry and curtail effectiveness? The real issue is obedience: Are leaders committed to obedience to scriptural truth, regardless of the consequences?

After being jailed, flogged, and intimidated, the apostles showed their spiritual fiber:

The apostles left the Sanhedrin, rejoicing because they had been counted worthy of suffering disgrace for the

Name. Day after day, in the temple courts and from house to house, they never stopped teaching and proclaiming the good news that Jesus is the Christ.

Acts 5:41, 42

They had no assurance of safety and never tried to rationalize backing off. Instead of indulging in self-pity, these men praised God for the opportunity they had and went back to work.

In our psychologized society, after such an attack, many of us would need two weeks in Tahoe, a prescription of Valium, and a full assessment before we could return to the task. Culture presents a full portfolio of excuses for disobedience. Take your pick: *I came from a dysfunctional family; my mother did it; my father did it; I had a mother; I had a father; I didn't have a mother; I didn't have a father; I have a disease; extensive testing shows my personality makes it impossible for me to obey God.*

While the above comments may have a sliver of truth to them, melted down and molded together they don't make an excuse for failing God. In the midst of the worst circumstances, God's perspective, learned on the field of obedience, keeps people faithful.

Stick to the Knitting

Acts 6 begins by describing another significant corrective measure. Again the apostles faced an internal problem, one that reveals the potential pettiness of God's people. The first section of the verse, "In those days when the number of disciples was increasing . . . ," only serves to make it that much more frustrating. When the ministry was really going strong, the enemy drove a wedge between people over the order of food distribution. (If you can't stop people from giving food, at least you can get them mad about the way it's served!) A conflict arose among the divergent groups of Jews over the neglect of some widows.

The apostles responded by gathering all the disciples. That doesn't mean they asked over 5,000 people to attend a church business meeting, but doubtless they invited key representatives from the two groups. Out of this meeting came two principles:

> Do not sacrifice your primary task to handle a secondary issue.
> Multiply yourself through others.

Do Not Sacrifice Your Primary Task to Handle a Secondary Issue. The apostles had learned this rule from Jesus. In Mark 1:35–39, Jesus was praying. When the disciples came looking for Him, with a view to returning to the immediate needs of the masses, Jesus surprised the twelve with his words: "Let us go somewhere else—to the nearby villages—so I can preach there also. That is why I have come" (Mark 1:38). This is but one example of many times when Jesus stuck to the knitting. He would not leave His main calling for a less important one.

Confronted with the food-distribution problem, the apostles declared their primary task: ". . . It would not be right for us to neglect the ministry of the word of God in order to wait on tables. . . . We will . . . give our attention to prayer and the ministry of the word" (Acts 6:2–4). They understood their calling, their task, and the best use of their gifts and time.

Today's pastor so badly needs this quality that I almost cannot overstate it. Not unusually, a pastor will tell me he is away from home five to seven nights a week. When I hear such a complaint, I retort: "You have lost control of your life. Others control you; you have lost sight of your calling, your gifts, and the ability to say no." When a pastor finds himself working an eighty-hour week, he is being a poor steward—of himself and of the people of the church.

Multiply Yourself Through Others. The apostles took the proper approach when they gave their decision to the disciples: "Choose seven men from among you who are known to be full of the Spirit and wisdom. We will turn this responsibility over to them" (Acts 6:3).

They had learned delegation from Jesus, too. When Jesus thought they were ready, He had multiplied Himself through the twelve, in order to meet a great variety of needs (Matthew 9:36–38; 10:1–42). The apostles turned the work over to men who were qualified and respected by the people, commissioning them by the laying on of hands. This gave the chosen men a sense of importance; they no longer felt like second-class Christians.

Outstandingly, the apostles passed along to the church Jesus' two management principles. They corrected this problem by means of them. When a leader can use those principles, he accomplishes three things:

He can stay true to his calling, and the work does not suffer.
He solves the problem in a way that brings long-term results.
He teaches the principles, passing them on to others.

As a by-product of such management, the confidence and competence of the congregation grow. It begins the process of full-bodied ministry that most powerfully expresses God's love.

Luke makes a supremely important connection when he says, "So the word of God spread. The number of disciples in Jerusalem increased rapidly, and a large number of priests became obedient to the faith" (Acts 6:7). The big word is "so." Because they handled the problem properly, the apostles could stick to the work, and God blessed it. The opposite could have happened—and usually does. If the pastor and church board allow internal squabbles and pettiness to capture them, they sabotage the ministry.

To halt such sabotage, the pastor must possess and practice the apostles' priorities. In the first church, because men of firm conviction handled corrective measures in a principled way, the work of God flourished.

THE REPRODUCTIVE STAGE

When 120 freshly filled believers spilled out of a stuffy Upper Room and preached the Gospel, it produced the first church. From 120 to 3,000 in one day is impressive conversion growth. Reproduction became normal at first church; members could not think of church without including daily witness. It had started with reproduction, and the church would live by this principle.

In today's climate, a church that experiences conversion growth without major outlay of funds for mega events is big news—write it up in Christian periodicals, interview the leaders on talk shows, invite them to speak at your conference. Put them on display, and tell them to write it down so others can learn how to do this! Though we *should* learn from such churches, how sad that despite the distinctiveness of reproduction, few churches experience conversions.

Before a church can reach the reproductive stage, it has to experience individual reproduction. People come to Christ through individual witness. Even though the first church started with reproduction and lived by it, it took time for the entire church to reach this stage. In the reproductive stage a church effectively combines its individual witness and corporate witness. The body must operate on all pistons, as described in Acts 2:42–47.

Corporate reproduction is not primarily church planting. Paul described it clearly when he said "each part does its work" (Ephesians 4:16). The difference between individual witness and corporate witness could be compared to the difference between a voice speaking words to you and an entire person with a body speaking to you. You need both the voice and the body, but the entire body at work has more impact.

How did the first church progress in its reproductive stage?

The Apostles Provided an Example

During the years described in the passage in Acts 2, the apostles preached and gave a daily witness. Even the threat of death did not alter their daily, unflagging commitment.

They continued to minister in the marketplace (Acts 4:33; 5:14, 21, 42).

Even after the dispersion, the twelve continued preaching and getting into trouble. Within the church, getting into this kind of trouble was esteemed. The congregation modeled itself on twelve men who made witness a part of daily life, and the body became reproductive.

If church leaders model committee meetings and paper shuffling as key activities, should anyone be surprised at local church anemia? Leaders who want church members to witness had better do it themselves. The contemporary church is light on conversions because leaders have cloistered themselves in the office—they no longer go out into the streets. If leaders don't evangelize, the possibility that the populace will becomes miniscule.

Reproduction of the Scattered Church

When the church was driven from Jerusalem, "those who had been scattered preached the word wherever they went" (Acts 8:4). They did what they had been taught, had seen, and what they considered normal.

As the maturation process unfolds across Acts 2–7, we see the reproductive process of the first church. The real proof came when persecution drove Christians from the city. The church reproduced by members' preaching wherever they went. The simple process of witness caused church planting through the general populace.

If you had asked the average member of the first church how to start a church, he would have answered, "Start preaching." Ask a contemporary believer, and you'll hear, "Form a committee."

To be fair, the first church didn't find the next stage, multiplication, natural; it came as the result of persecution. Early believers felt no more inclined to leave friends and security of a marvelous spiritual environment than most modern believers would. Leaving a comfort zone has never been easy, even for the most Spartan believers.

Philip preached in Samaria; Peter ventured to the house of Cornelius; Saul became Paul. Persecution scattered the first church, and key figures traveled to unreached areas. Eventually the first church would have accomplished all this, but waiting for the flesh to agree with the Spirit would have taken too long; the mission was critical enough to require immediate intervention—persecution.

The founding of the church at Antioch most impressively demonstrates the multiplication that followed:

> Now those who had been scattered by the persecution in connection with Stephen traveled as far as Phoenicia, Cyprus and Antioch, *telling the message only to Jews.* Some of them, however, *men from Cyprus and Cyrene,* went to Antioch and began to speak to Greeks also, telling them the good news about the Lord Jesus. The Lord's hand was with them, and a great number of people believed and turned to the Lord.
>
> Acts 11:19–21, *italics added*

The Gentiles got into the preaching loop without official first-church certification or strategic planning. We see the power of the model of reproduction: If you multiply a reproductive church, it creates other reproductive churches. This will remain true until modeling breaks down.

The first church is an impressive model for all churches. It shows the disciples' first application of Jesus' teaching and strategy.

6
Breaking the Barriers to Disciple Making

Even though a church reaches the great heights of the first church, if it does not push on spiritually, the body slowly loses energy. By forcing it from Jerusalem, God kept the first church vital, yet thirty years later, the letter to the Hebrews indicates the same believers had regressed theologically and functionally. The once-effective people had to return to the ABCs of Christian teaching that they had known when God dispersed them.

INSTITUTIONALISM: ENEMY OF CHANGE

When God moved the first church out of Jerusalem, it had working capital of over 10,000 Christians cooped up in the city. Because the congregation faced the imminent danger of becoming a religious institution He could not use, God sent the first church packing.

The fledgling church could not have anticipated the great geographic, financial, and racial barriers it would face. In order to continue making disciples and spreading the Gospel, believers would have to overcome all these barriers and a greater one—human nature.

The adventurous Pilgrims who braved the tumultuous Atlantic Ocean made major sacrifices before and during the voyage to their new land. As they settled, these brave men and women fought disease, cruel winters, hostile Indians, and internal bickering. Their champion spirits won, and they established a new community.

After establishing a sense of normalcy in the community, a few Pilgrims wanted to press inland, to develop new areas. Almost unanimously, the people who had settled the New World rejected the plan as too difficult—they had become institutionalized. Institutionalism is hardening of the categories.

Institute something, and you act progressively, even daringly. Following an idea's birth, a movement forms around it, and a dynamic environment results. But without authority structure and rules, such a fast-moving organism will destroy itself. So you establish some guidelines.

Time passes, and the authority structure, rules, and methods find their niches. A movement started by ideologues who challenged structures and demanded change now resists change. For example, look at Steve Jobs, the whiz kid behind Apple's MacIntosh. He started Apple with vision and ideals. When it became a major corporation with institutional characteristics, Jobs struggled with the environment. The rules finally caused him to leave the organization he founded.

Though instituting is good and institutions are fine, institutionalism cripples progress. It resists change and slows down or even punishes innovative minds and spirits. This absolutely normal, predictable, but difficult-to-recognize process may most blind those who were once its greatest visionaries.

According to Hebrews 5:11—6:4, the first church eventually suffered from crippling institutionalism. But the problem may already have existed when the church was scattered. People could already have felt satisfied with the way things were. They had found their comfort zone.

Few people ever perceive they are ready to do the hard thing. The Jerusalem Christians had the security of a magnetic community and leaders who had walked with Christ. Knowing that to open up new areas of witness would probably bring on the same persecution that the apostles had experienced, maybe they didn't feel ready for such a change. Normal human tendencies may have slowed the first church's inauguration of outreach. I believe they had no dispersal plans on the drawing board. If they had, God's intervention would have been needless. God's expansion plan called for an early launch. So He smashed the barrier to outreach in a way that gave the people little choice: They could go to jail, be stoned to death, or leave town (Acts 8:1, 2).

Previous persecution had pulled the church together; now it pulled it apart for evangelism. God's plan called for a much wider scattering than man's best plan could have devised. Apart from the twelve, how many Christians could have been motivated to leave for evangelistic purposes? Even if only 50 percent of the scattered shared their faith, with His plan, a few thousand preached Christ to the world.

Barrier Breaker: Decentralization

Scattering the believers resulted in a decentralized ministry no longer threatened by institutionalism. When the majority of the congregation left Jerusalem, the apostles did not rush out to join them. I believe they remained because they could. After the Ananias and Sapphira episode, even the officials feared harming the twelve. Jewish authorities placed wetted fingers in the air and decided the winds of popularity blew too strongly to allow them to attack Peter and company.

By staying in Jerusalem, the apostles also affirmed three building blocks of decentralized ministry.

1. Everyone Is Called to Ministry. The apostles felt confident that God had called the ordinary believer to ministry. Their Teacher had shown them people were more capable than they expected to be; though Christians might not know as much as they thought, they could do more than they believed they could.

2. Without Multiplication, You Cannot Have Decentralization of Ministry. The twelve *could* have gone along, and from time to time they would venture out, but staying in Jerusalem provided a natural way for reproduction and multiplication to occur. As long as they were not around, the average Christian felt free to take on larger tasks. As a result, more people could be reached with the Gospel.

3. Training Christians or Making Disciples Must Precede Meaningful Multiplication or Decentralization. The Christians who left Jerusalem had been well taught, and they followed up on their lessons. "Those who had been scattered preached the word of God wherever they went" (Acts 8:4). Their actions proved the apostles' convictions concerning decentralization:

> Communicating the faith was not regarded as the preserve of the very zealous or the officially designated evangelist. Evangelism was the prerogative and the duty of every Church member. We have seen apostles and wandering prophets, nobles and paupers, intellectuals and fishermen all taking part enthusiastically in this primary task committed by Christ to his Church. The ordinary people of the Church saw it as their job: Christianity was supremely a lay movement, spread by informal missionaries.[1]

Breaking Down the Barriers

For the first church, breaking down institutionalism's barriers meant overcoming fear and resistance to change, and leaving the comfortable niches they had dug in a vibrant community. It meant facing persecution without the apostles' presence and discarding old methods that worked in Jerusalem, but not in Judea; it was ministry without a net.

God broke the barriers by throwing Christians in the water: "Go ahead, swim, the water is fine." In the face of persecution, the laity became a decentralized ministry that proved its worth in the results of the preaching of the scattered church.

By following the guidelines of the first church, the contemporary church can also break down institutionalism's barriers.

The Church Must Resist Institutionalism. The modern church is more mired in institutionalism than its first-century counterpart. Whereas the early Christian resisted change because he experienced a vibrant, caring environment, today many resist expansion because it threatens their power base. Though a cold, resistant organization may look like a church, sound like a church, and think it is a church, it is not one. People may not even like such an imitation product, yet they fight tooth and nail to keep what they hate. Somewhere in the depths of this organization a real church *may* exist, but you'd need archaeological tools to find it.

When people find their niche in a church and stay there, they enter the comfort zone. Nothing challenges their fears, confronts them with their weaknesses, or asks them to expand their strengths. The key word is *sameness,* and the patron saint of the comfort zone is Walter Mitty. Though comfort-zone Christians may dream about change, they awake to major realities that prove too tough to battle. They resist the push to expand or be creative by answering calls to fine-tune the institutional machinery. People become too comfortable with their leaders, roles, and mediocrity.

Keeping the vision before the people breaks the back of institutionalism. Challenge them to face their fears and work on their weaknesses—and more important, to find and develop their strengths. Encourage them to move into their strong points, and keep the organization in motion.

The Church Must Be Vigilant to Expand Through the Common Believer. For a short time after the dispersion of the church, God kept the apostles in Jerusalem. Their presence in the field would have intimidated less experienced Christians and sabotaged God's plan. Many would have deferred to the twelve. It's the same when a pastor attends a lay-led Bible study. His appearance alters the actions of the leader and the group dynamic. The vital key to God's plan is that the laity does the work—as well as the apostles or the pastor would do it.

The contemporary church has some erroneous ideas about ministry. Simultaneously Christians entertain the conflicting concepts that the pastor alone can do important spiritual work and that God equally values all believers.

Correctly they believe that every member has a gift and ministry to contribute to the church, and everyone must work together to make the body effective. But rather than following this to its logical conclusion, they take 75 percent of the possible ministry and shove it into a professional minister's portfolio, leaving the second-class evangelical chores for themselves.

As the pastor struggles to give ministry away, a poorly trained congregation fallaciously sees his giving away important work as sheer pastoral laziness or complains that he gives away the "dirty work."

Congregations expect pastors to do numerous "holy jobs": baptism, serving communion, pastoral prayer, visiting the sick, counseling, leading board meetings, and leading Wednesday-night services. At one time or another, every pastor does these tasks, but not one of the above tasks *needs* to be done by the pastor. Scripture does not associate any of these more with the clergy than the congregation. A full-bodied ministry will engage clergy and nonclergy alike in such tasks.

Take the classic example of hospital visitation. Visiting the sick is a ministry given to the entire body. The Bible gives no evidence that this is the pastor's job, yet even when the laity *do* visit the sick, counsel the bereaved, or intervene in a crisis, everyone expects the pastor to duplicate the task. If ten lay ministers visit a hospitalized person, but the pastor does not, will that person complain he has not been visited? What is he saying? That only the pastor's ministry is worthwhile; parishioner ministry isn't good enough. Only certain visits count.

To paraphrase Paul's command in 1 Corinthians 12, the hand should not say to the foot, "I have no need of you," or, "Because you are not a hand, you are less important." When a layman does a traditional pastoral duty, requiring it to be redone by a professional is a rejection of that layperson. In effect, the ministered-to Christian says, "I will not receive the ministry of others in the body. Theirs is only a token, not the real McCoy."

This serious barrier needs smashing, because it has caused the church to become poisoned by institutionalism and hinders its work. Many hurting, broken pastors have been driven out of the ministry by such unreasonable congregational demands. They want to train God's people to be effective ministers, as Ephesians 4:11–16 has called them to. They want to create loving, caring environments where Christians excel and begin to make their lives count for Christ. But how can pastors do this when churches won't allow it? Can one man preach Sunday morning, Sunday night, and Wednesday night; attend committee meetings, Sunday-school socials, and denominational meetings; and still do all the counseling and administration of the church? *No!*

Nothing will change for overworked pastors until a courageous few lead the charge for change. I can almost guarantee the situation will get worse before it gets better, but making that change will be worth the pain, trouble, and time. Pastors must be freed from oppressive expectations and work loads so they can obey God.

The expansion of God's work requires the unleashing of the laity; the concept of *laity* must be abolished, and people must be liberated to do important spiritual work, including counseling, teaching, evangelizing, caring for the sick, baptizing converts, and serving communion to those entrusted to their care.

Pastors need to move over and tell the congregation, "You are ministers/pastors, too. There is room on the pedestal for you." Better yet, throw away the pedestals. But whether you bring others up to your level or go down to theirs, the change needs to be made. The up and down of the ministry is a cultural curse, manufactured by inflated egos and scriptural ignorance.

I believe the maxim "The cause of every problem is change" is true. Institutionalism's greatest fear is change. To break the barrier, create change. God did that by creating new workers, who became the new leaders, spearheading the Gospel.

GEOGRAPHIC AND RACIAL PREJUDICE: ENEMIES OF MISSION

Beyond the barrier of institutionalism, the growing church faced prejudice. *Webster's Dictionary* defines *prejudice* as a "preconceived preference or bias. To possess an irrational hatred of a particular group, race, or religion."

The first church believed two things: They were the best and most favored of people in the world; and the most important—and holy—city and land were Jerusalem and Israel. They had been brought up to believe these things, and their attendance at the feast of Pentecost substantiates their adherence to these beliefs.

The first church would have hesitated to accept two groups in their midst. *Hesitate* is actually a nice way to say the genetically pure Jew considered half-breeds and Gentiles as spiritual left-outs. They were not part of the promise to Abraham—they were dogs, the scum of the earth, and God used them only to serve the Jewish people.

If first church was to obey God, to take the Gospel to Judea, Samaria, and the remotest parts of the earth, the prejudice barrier needed smashing. Once again God broke the barrier. He sent Philip to Samaria, Peter to Cornelius's house, and Paul to the Gentiles. Philip went to the half-breeds because he was the least bigoted. God sent Peter to Cornelius because he was the most prejudiced. Well-educated Paul went to the multilayered, complex Gentile population.

Philip's Visit to Samaria

Philip, a Hellenistic Jew, had been educated and influenced by Greek culture. That would have made it easier for him to accept those of the "corrupted" gene pool—the Samaritans.

The Samaritans were a product of Israel's disobedience. The northern ten tribes had separated from Judah and Benjamin. When the Assyrian Empire overran them, they intermarried. Genetically pure Jews snubbed these half-breeds and had nothing to do with them. Many Jews would not even travel through Samaria.

Not bothered by such parochial attitudes, Philip plowed ahead and preached with great success. "When crowds heard Philip and saw the miraculous signs he did, they all paid close attention to what he said. With shrieks, evil spirits came out of many, and many paralytics and cripples were healed. So there was great joy in that city" (Acts 8:6–8).

For the first time—or *any* time—out, Philip did well. Philip's ministry had all the markings of legitimacy: He verbalized the faith, the power of God was demonstrated, many believed, and there was joy. People could hear it, see it, act on it, and feel it.

John Wesley measured his sermons by two standards: Were people converted, and was anyone angered? By this rule, Philip was successful. Not only did people come to Christ, but conflict followed Philip as Simon the sorcerer alternately opposed and followed him.

A Window on Accountability. The apostles sent Peter and John to check out Philip's budding ministry. Though they wanted to multiply their efforts, the twelve also wanted quality control. They needed evidence that God's hand was in the Samaritans' acceptance of Christ.

Surely Peter and John spoke with converts, questioning them concerning their decisions. To be sure God had broken down this barrier, they would pray for the Samaritans to receive the Holy Spirit the way they had received Him. So they prayed, and the Samaritans received the Spirit, praising God in unknown tongues. Evidence of the powerful results can be seen in Simon's response: ". . . Simon saw that the Spirit was given at the laying on of the apostles' hands . . ." (Acts 8:18).

God had confirmed the destruction of the Samaritan barrier; the reality of His power could not be denied. On the basis of this, Peter and John preached on their way home, through Samaritan cities. Their actions reflected a major change in their worldview.

Whenever the church multiplies ministry, delegated authority requires accountability. Without it, multiplied ministry is trouble looking for a place to happen. Pollution of the message, imitation of methods, misappropriation of gifts, and financial corruption are but a few hazards slackness courts.

Let's suppose a sweater manufacturer wanted to reproduce thousands of the same item. If they have several factories, they had better possess specifications concerning quality control, or in a short time they won't recognize their product.

Paul called the Gospel a "sacred deposit" (2 Timothy 1:14). Its purity is preeminent. All early church authority followed a simple progression of delegation. Ultimate authority rested in Christ: ". . . All authority in heaven and on earth has been given to me" (Matthew 28:18). He delegated that authority to the apostles: "Therefore go and make disciples of all nations . . ." (Matthew 28:19). Acts 1:8 provides the apostles' strategy and geographic authority. The apostles, including Paul, delegated this to elders in local churches (Acts 14:23). When Paul realized he would not return to Ephesus, he charged the church's leaders to take over permanently (Acts 20:28). The counsel at Jerusalem (Acts 15) and the reporting Paul did to the Jerusalem church demonstrate the existence of and respect for a total authority structure over each church and the entire, combined church.

Peter Visits Cornelius

Peter illustrates the best and worst of all disciples: He could see over the horizon one day and not beyond his nose the next; he was both proud and prejudiced. As point man for the disciples, not surprisingly he was one of the first to go on a preaching mission, about a year after the church scattered.

To break the racial/geographical barrier, God's ministry point man had to be convinced in a dramatic experience. Philip's powerful ministry had adjusted Peter's attitude toward reaching the Samaritans. On their way back to Jerusalem, he and John preached to Samaritan cities. When Peter set out on his own preaching mission, he went to a town just northwest of Jerusalem, Lydda. He preached so successfully that all those living in Lydda and Sharon who saw the healed man, Aeneas, turned to the Lord (Acts 9:32–35). Peter traveled on to Joppa and raised Tabitha from the dead. Many heard of this and believed on Christ (9:36–42). No one felt surprised that Peter had been mightily used by God.

But the stubborn apostle, slow to unlearn some things, had a serious shock: God appeared to him and clearly told him to preach the Gospel to the Gentiles (Acts 10:9–16). He was sent to the house of a Gentile believer named Cornelius, who had experienced a similar vision.

Peter introduced himself and began to explain why he was breaking Jewish law by associating with Gentiles: ". . . God has shown me that I should not call any man impure or unclean. . . . I now realize how true it is that God does not show favoritism' " (Acts 10:28, 34). Peter began to preach, but never finished his sermon:

> While Peter was still speaking these words, the Holy
> Spirit came on all who heard the message. The

circumcised believers who had come with Peter were astonished that the gift of the Holy Spirit had been poured out even on the Gentiles. For they heard them speaking in tongues and praising God.

Acts 10:44–46

When God has quick change as His priority, he puts His people on the fast track. Instead of waiting for Peter to learn about prejudice, God smashed the barrier in fifteen minutes. Peter was ready to accept that God loved the Gentiles and wanted the Gospel preached to them. But all—including the other Jews with Peter—were flabbergasted when God gave them tongues. Through the common experience of speaking in tongues, God showed Peter that His Spirit was poured out on three groups: the Jews, the Samaritans, and the Gentiles. Just a few months before, they had been separated by hundreds of years of mutual loathing, but God made these peoples one in Christ.

God used two main tools to break the barriers. First, he convinced His key representative, through dramatic vision or revelation. Next, an unmistakable sign of His power authenticated the change.

The Apostles' Acceptance. How much trouble did the apostles have accepting this "new blood"? "The apostles and the brothers throughout Judea heard that the Gentiles also had received the word of God. So when Peter went up to Jerusalem, the circumcised believers criticized him and said, 'You went into the house of uncircumcised men and ate with them' " (Acts 11:1–3).

Only one thing would convince the apostles: the same thing that worked on Peter. Hardheaded, pragmatic men, they wanted some evidence that the paradigm shift came from God.

Peter simply told his story, including the vision and miracle of the Holy Spirit being poured out on Cornelius and company. Powerfully, he concluded: " 'So if God gave them the same gift as he gave us, who believed in the Lord Jesus Christ, who was I to think that I could oppose God?" (Acts 11:17).

Careful to test all matters and take leadership responsibility seriously, the apostles still remained open to God's Spirit. They agreed with Peter: "When they heard this, they had no further objections and praised God . . ." (Acts 11:18). Though affected by culture and tradition, the apostles' spiritual character allowed them to change attitudes when God spoke. How rare this quality is in the contemporary church!

Are We Breaking the Barriers?

For most Christians, the racial barrier is not an intellectual one. The average white evangelical says, "I would accept a black or other minority who attended my church." I believe he means that, but to what degree would he be willing to live in community with minority members?

Actually the socioeconomic barrier looms larger than the racial one. Most local churches attract people from a single community that represents a single economic strata. Upper middle class people mix easily, regardless of race, because other common denominators unify them. Sharing community with a person of another race and more meager economic and educational means presents greater problems. However, in most local churches, the opportunity for mixing races and economic stratas remain remote.

More relevantly, are we willing to move into different cultures, live among them, and share the Gospel? Are there any unclean ones to whom we will not minister? Are we willing to hear God's voice? The words of Peter stand true today, "Who was I to think that I could oppose God?"

MOVING MECCA: A NEW SENDING CENTER

Naturally the first church grew up in Jerusalem, the Holy City. But an expanding church meant change. Part of that change included a shift of the center of action. Though

Jerusalem remained the mother church, as time passed it became more of a maintenance ministry.

God called a new apostle, named Paul, to preach to the Gentile world. The center of action moved to wherever he happened to be. By raising up another man whose gifts, educational background, and personality would make him effective in a cosmopolitan mission field, God pushed the church off center and out into the world.

Preaching Without Portfolio

> Now those who had been scattered by the persecution in connection with Stephen traveled as far as Phoenicia, Cyprus and Antioch, telling the message only to the Jews. Some of them, however, men from Cyprus and Cyrene, went to Antioch and began to speak to Greeks also, telling them the good news about the Lord Jesus. The Lord's hand was with them, and a great number of people believed and turned to the Lord.
>
> Acts 11:19–21

When new believers get too far away from the mother institution, they start unauthorized evangelism; it is the kind of insubordination the church desperately needs. These dispersed Christians broke rank much the way a soldier steps from dress parade to save a drowning swimmer. The nonordained became more fruitful than anyone would have thought.

Tongue in cheek, some have said we should not introduce new believers to older ones, because the new ones might find out that they don't really need to witness. Such sarcasm holds more truth than we'd like to admit. New believers given basic instructions often apply them pristinely. Without question they start doing the obvious, important things. Easily we can understand how the enthusiasm of new life in Christ, unencumbered by institutional Christianity, led to fruitful ministry. The early Christians did not hesitate to cross racial, geographic, and religious boundaries.

Barnabas and Paul

Upon hearing of the Spirit's movement in Antioch through unknown disciples, the apostles sent Joseph of Cyprus, nicknamed *Barnabas*, to check it out. This man, known for his ability to encourage, exhort, and build people up in the faith, had the trust of both the apostles and the people. He possessed integrity and sensitivity. Barnabas had used those gifts when he brought the very dangerous convert Saul of Tarsus to Jerusalem and introduced him to the apostles, to authenticate his conversion. He put Saul into good relationship with the angry, frightened people who knew of Saul's persecution of the church and his role in the killing of Stephen. Ironically, the man who headed the persecution would become a convert and disciple of those he scattered.

The sending of Barnabas to Antioch demonstrates three discipling principles.

1. Multiplication Had Created the Need for Someone to Visit Antioch.

Fruitful preaching of the "men from Cyprus and Cyrene" gave birth to the Antioch church. As the mother church, Jerusalem had the responsibility to oversee this congregation.

2. The Apostles Sent Barnabas Because Effective Multiplication Always Includes Quality Control Through Accountability.

Not only were the apostles curious, they wanted to insure the quality of message and messengers. *Who are these preachers without portfolios? What are they teaching? Are they carrying on the priorities and practices of the first church?* These are vital concerns, and the establishment of authority and accountability in the new church would set its course for many years to come.

3. The Choice of Barnabas Exemplifies Use of the Right Gifts for the Right Situation.

These new Christians needed to be encouraged, built up, and taught. The man sent from headquarters had to establish rapport with the new believers—and Barnabas was just the man for that job.

Quickly passing through Antioch, Barnabas moved on to Tarsus, to pick up Paul. The apostle had been "on ice" for nearly fourteen years. In our environment, we find it hard to believe anyone with Paul's ability would have lain on the shelf for this long. But don't assume, simply because Paul was back in Tarsus, that he did not preach, learn, and do the work of the ministry. Not preaching would have gone against Paul's personality flow.

As talented and dynamic as Paul was, without Barnabas, he would have failed. Barnabas saved Paul's bacon several times. When he brought Paul to Antioch, Barnabas considered this a good time to break Paul in at a church other than Jerusalem. Paul didn't fit in at the first church, where there were too many important people around. He was in a special category and needed "ministry space."

The mission at Antioch became a tremendous success. ". . . So for a whole year Barnabas and Saul met with the church and taught great numbers of people. The disciples were called Christians first at Antioch" (Acts 11:26).

The Completed Transition

By leading them over difficult barriers that threatened growth, God saved the first church from institutionalism. We can see the result in the maturity of the Antioch church. Eventually the upstart congregation at Antioch found itself in a unique position: It could help the first church. Just as children reach a great family moment when they can help their parents, Antioch's helping the first church marked a milestone in Christianity's expansion.

Jerusalem's prophets prophesied a famine. Antioch responded immediately: "The disciples, each according to his ability, decided to provide help for the brothers living in Judea. This they did, sending their gift to the elders by Barnabas and Saul" (Acts 11:29, 30). Until now, Jerusalem had always given, and Antioch received. God worked this crisis according to His plan, and the Antioch church learned to give, while Jerusalem received. Antioch needed to feel grown up; it was essential to its new role and status for the church to know it could hear from God and take action.

After a couple of years, the Antioch church had elders; they were well taught and thinking mission. Remember, Paul took in all he heard and saw. The influence of the first church on Antioch, through Barnabas, and Barnabas's influence on Paul set the priorities and practices for future Pauline church plants.

While the center of authority stayed in Jerusalem, the center of mission moved to Antioch. The apostles had the commission and authority, but Antioch had the God-ordained evangelist to the Gentiles. Antioch would become the cutting edge for mission, the mission station.

Barnabas and Paul seemed submissive to the Antioch elders. At the end of Acts 12, we find a revealing comment: "When Barnabas and Saul had finished their mission, they returned from Jerusalem, taking with them John, also called Mark" (v. 25). These men did not stay at the first church, the center of all authority, the center of quality control. Jerusalem had become a modality—a mature institution that requires a great deal of maintenance. Though alive, first church labored under a tremendous administrative load, like all mature organizations. The modality must keep spinning off sodalities, fast-moving, vision-driven mission groups, unencumbered by heavy maintenance needs.

Antioch had become what first church had been. Pulsating with new life, it made new rules nearly as fast as it broke them. First church, still alive and exciting, required that much of its leadership and labor focus on maintenance. Antioch took up the mantle of mission. Located at the edge of the unreached world, with the apostle Paul at its service, it had everything needed—including the direction of God. "In the church at Antioch there were prophets and teachers . . . ," Luke says (Acts 13:1). The church had grown in numbers and ministry ability; spiritual gifts had been discovered and developed.

As the people worshiped the Lord and fasted, the Lord

clearly spoke: "Set apart for me Barnabas and Saul for the work to which I have called them" (v. 2). God called the leaders to make known before the entire church that he had called Barnabas and Paul to mission. Laying on of hands indicated a transfer of authority from the elders to the evangelists, for a certain work. God wanted the entire church to understand the significance of their mission: The two men went out with the blessing and authority of the church. In this exciting moment, the first church's first major outpost intentionally deployed trained leaders who went out to reproduce and multiply.

Part III

THE MISSION CHURCH

In Antioch Barnabas had taught Paul the practices and principles of the first church. Now together they move out on a missionary journey that will bring the Gospel to Galatia. Preaching to Jew and Gentile, they begin to learn new techniques of founding and strengthening congregations. As they travel, the ministry of the apostle to the Gentiles becomes increasingly clear.

In the second journey, Paul, no longer an apprentice, reproduces all he has learned. The Gospel spreads to Macedonia and Corinth in his second and third missions, and the church continues to grow. Through the account in Acts and through his letters to the congregations founded during the missionary journeys we can learn more of what it takes to make a discipling church. Here, in the fertile ground of the Gentiles, the church effectively reproduces itself—despite opposition, problems, and a once seemingly impossible task.

7
The Early Mission Church Meets Jesus

On his first two mission tours, Paul planted more than fifteen churches. Because it is the first application of discipling churches in non-Hebraic cultures, I have named this conglomerate the *mission church*. It bridged various languages, cultures, and religious environments and represents the best church-planting curriculum.

Paul's first tour lasted two years and included eight cities. Luke covers the mission in eighty verses (Acts 13:1—14:28). For the first church this step was multiplication, and for Antioch it was reproduction. For Paul and Barnabas it was formative work: They had to feel their way along and creatively contextualize their principles.

As with any other church, the mission church went through the four-stage process of "Come and see," "Come and follow me," "Come and be with Me," and "Remain in Me" (*see* Chart 5). Journey one was "Come and see," the

Chart 5
The Mission Church

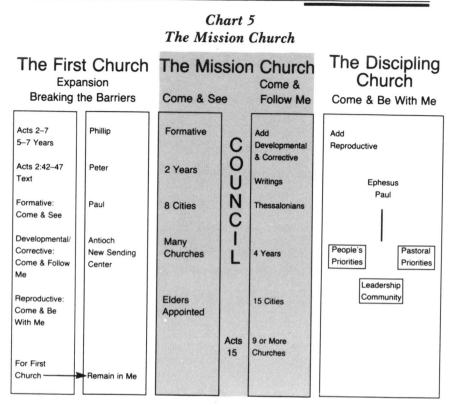

The First Church Expansion Breaking the Barriers		The Mission Church Come & See		Come & Follow Me	The Discipling Church Come & Be With Me
Acts 2–7 5–7 Years	Phillip	Formative	C	Add Developmental & Corrective	Add Reproductive
Acts 2:42–47 Text	Peter	2 Years	O U	Writings	
Formative: Come & See	Paul	8 Cities	N C	Thessalonians	Ephesus Paul
Developmental/ Corrective: Come & Follow Me	Antioch New Sending Center	Many Churches	I L	4 Years	People's Priorities Pastoral Priorities
Reproductive: Come & Be With Me		Elders Appointed		15 Cities	Leadership Community
For First Church ──────▶	Remain in Me		Acts 15	9 or More Churches	

formative stage. Journey two adds the developmental stage, "Come and follow Me," combined with some corrective action. In the third journey, Paul added reproduction and leadership development, the "Come and be with Me" stage. "Remain in Me" took place when Paul spent four years in prison, and his staff took on the oversight responsibilities.

Every church should set the continual development through these stages as its goal. But instead of making the journeys of Paul the journey of their church, most congregations stall out in one of the first two stages.

THE FIRST JOURNEY'S STRATEGIES

From Jesus the apostles had learned to go where the people were. So daily the first church prayed and preached in the temple, the center of religious discussion, where people converged. Barnabas would have passed this technique along to Antioch, where he ministered with Paul, and Paul learned to apply it and in turn passed it on to the mission church.

Within the first mission, we see Paul facing two distinct audiences, and he treated them differently in order to reach each with the Gospel. He began with the Jews, using a strategy keyed to their needs and background.

Synagogue Strategy
Wherever ten believing Jewish families existed, they could form a synagogue. Therefore Paul started his penetration in this prepared ground at Salamis, Pisidian Antioch, Iconium, and perhaps other cities.

> The synagogue provided the seedbed for evangelism among the Jews. Wherever there were Jews, there were synagogues, and all loyal Israelites were expected to attend weekly; furthermore, they attracted a number of godfearers among thoughtful Gentiles. Here was a ready made congregation for Christian missionaries to address.[1]

As a matter of custom, the synagogue offered opportunity for visiting teachers to present a message.[2] Luke details the request for a message of encouragement made in the synagogue at Pisidian Antioch (Acts 13:15), and Paul's sermon gives a model of a message contextualized for his audience (13:16–41). In a Jewish history lesson that taps into his auditors' belief system, Paul identifies with them and pulls the Jews along to his predetermined destination. Well received, he and Barnabas were asked back next week. "On the next Sabbath almost the whole city gathered to hear the word of the Lord. When the Jews saw the crowds, they were filled with jealousy and talked abusively against what Paul was saying" (Acts 13:44, 45).

They invited Paul back because of their true interest in his message, but their curiosity crumbled beneath the flesh. No high or theological reasons caused them to reject Paul's preaching; instead the high attendance he commanded smashed their egos.

More than pragmatism drove Paul's synagogue strategy. He held to the "to the Jew first" preaching order (Romans 1:16). ". . . We had to speak the word of God to you first. Since you reject it and do not consider yourselves worthy of eternal life, we now turn to the Gentiles" (Acts 13:46, 47). Unless God led differently, Paul preached first in the synagogue. Jesus practiced this when He sent the twelve first to Israel (Matthew 10:1–42). Initially the first church had gone to the temple. Paul followed suit, but if the Jews rejected him, he felt free to move to more fertile ground.

From the synagogue strategy, we can develop some helpful principles for today's church:

1. Target your prime candidates and go where they are.
2. When you go, make certain you clearly communicate the message.
3. If people respond well, stay and work with them, but if they reject the message, move on to more fertile ground.

The Gentile Strategy

When he left the Jews for the Gentiles, Paul began by establishing a beachhead, a place where he could dig into enemy territory. In Athens he went to the marketplace; elsewhere he worked from the home of a sympathetic family. Using a wide variety of methods—open-air preaching, teaching evangelism, testimony, house-to-house visitation, and so on—Paul and Barnabas began to spread the Gospel.

On the island of Cyprus, in their first mission, the two men encountered a Jewish sorcerer named Bar-Jesus. When Bar-Jesus opposed the evangelists' preaching, Paul blinded him, and the proconsul, before whom they had been speaking, believed (Acts 13:6–12). In most places, miracles substantiated the first preaching of Christ. Primarily this supported His claim to deity. Today, on mission fields where Christ's deity remains unestablished, miracles still take place, though they may not always occur as intentionally as this one.

After visiting Iconium and being run out by Jews who refused to believe and "poisoned their minds" (Acts 14:2), the pair moved on to Lystra and Derbe, using every available preaching method.

Lystra. A personal encounter served as Lystra's beachhead, when Paul healed a crippled man. The people responded with fanatical adulation and a riot, as they named Paul and Barnabas gods. As the crowds came bearing gifts and animals for sacrifice, Paul and Barnabas would have none of it. They tore their clothes to communicate their unhappiness to the thousands of screaming fans.

Paul seized the moment and launched into a sermon. This message differed vastly from the ones he had given to the Jews. The Gentiles didn't possess the tradition of the Torah or the oral history of the Jewish people; they understood their own gods, their work, their culture. Paul packaged this message for clean theological slates, contextualizing it to their understanding. He mentioned how rain helps crops, providing food and making everyone happy. This goodness, he explained, comes from a caring God. Even at that, the evangelists had a difficult time stopping the sacrifices.

But opposition followed them. The Jews from Antioch and Iconium incited the crowd against Paul and Barnabas, and they stoned Paul and left him for dead outside the town.

Derbe. After the eventful experience at Lystra, the mission at Derbe seems almost tame. "They preached the good news in that city and won a large number of disciples . . ." (Acts 14:21). Normally they entered a city and took whatever came. The mission at Cyprus had involved a healed man and a blinded sorcerer, which brought a backlash. Nothing so dangerous happened at Derbe.

THE FIRST JOURNEY'S RESULTS

People Were Converted

In every case of this mission, we have evidence that people converted to Christ. In Cyprus the proconsul listened, watched, and accepted Christ. In Pisidian Antioch, the evangelists were invited to speak again. After the first meeting, many wanted to talk to Paul and Barnabas. The next sabbath began the conversion of the Gentiles: "When the Gentiles heard this, they were glad and honored the word of the Lord; and all who were appointed for eternal life believed" (Acts 13:48). From this beachhead the word spread through the whole region. As a result "the disciples were filled with joy and with the Holy Spirit" (Acts 13:52).

In Iconium an unusually large number—both Jews and Gentiles—believed. Paul and Barnabas spent considerable time there, speaking boldly for the Lord, who confirmed the message of His grace by enabling them to do miraculous signs and wonders.

The purely Gentile missions, in Lystra and Derbe, bore fruit as well.

Opposition Arose

As surely as preaching leads to conversion, it leads to opposition: Bar-Jesus in Cyprus, the religious establishment in Pisidian Antioch, and the Jews of Iconium, who objected to the message and, along with others, followed the evangelists to Lystra, to cause trouble. In Iconium, where both Jews and Gentiles believed, the evangelists' popularity in synagogue and marketplace was only partial: "The people of the city were divided; some sided with the Jews, others with the apostles" (Acts 14:4).

Opposition is normal, and only the naive cry foul when they receive unfair treatment. Many well-meaning people have fallen for myths that a good church is trouble free, lines up perfectly behind the pastor's ideas, and never fights. When trouble comes, these naive Christians begin to believe that someone is out of God's will. That someone, I believe, is usually Satan. If trouble means you're out of God's will, Paul and Barnabas must have been out of His will, along with the apostles, most of the prophets, and Jesus Himself.

Though many modern Christian leaders teach a lack of conflict is the signpost of proper Christianity, I believe conflict is normal to effective ministry. Though I hate conflict, I suggest that those who want to obey God learn to live with it.

In the first century the Gospel was clean and clear. Satan opposed the church with riots, stonings, confrontations, and the like. The early church, an upstart, outsider, and threat to the religious establishment of its day faced outside opposition. Today's church, as the religious establishment, receives opposition as part of its factory equipment. Satan does a very effective inside job.

When the church populace begins to spread lies concerning your character, or the board keeps turning down your plans for change, don't cry foul. Satan uses many subversive, insidious means to divide the church: everything from the elders fighting the trustees, to the women's missionary society warring with the Kids Klubs' leaders to keep the youngsters out of the church kitchen. If the enemy can get church members to fight against one another, they won't have the time, energy, or disposition to love the world. Part of winning this battle involves focusing on your strengths, working hard on your objectives, and not allowing yourself to get distracted. Think of conflict as normal, and you can emotionally adjust and continue to concentrate on the mission.

Not only did Paul and Barnabas see opposition as normal, they considered it a sure sign of success. The belief had begun with Jesus' teachings, was practiced by the early church, and had become a cardinal truth of the church (Matthew 5:11, 12; Acts 4:25–32; 13:26–28). The new church clearly taught ". . . We must go through many hardships to enter the kingdom of God" (Acts 14:22).

Leaders may stir up opposition in two ways. The first is by obeying God and leading the church according to God's agenda. This creates a great deal of friction. The other way is to be passive and allow the church to stagnate. This method causes the congregation to criticize the pastor for his lack of leadership. Either way, leadership faces opposition, so why not make your opposition count?

Paul and Barnabas picked their opponents well. Like them, make your enemies those who oppose the Gospel. Go forward, preach everywhere, don't be deterred.

Churches Were Planted

On this first missionary journey, Paul and Barnabas traveled for two years. The first year they went out, and the second they returned home. On the way out, they primarily evangelized; on the way back, they began the formative stage in the churches they had founded, giving some attention to the development of leaders. At Derbe "they preached the good news in that city and won a large number of disciples. Then they returned to Lystra, Iconium and Antioch, strengthening the disciples and encouraging them to remain true to the faith" (Acts 14:21, 22). Later writings, such as the letter to the Galatians, addressed to Pisidian Antioch, Iconium, Lystra, and Derbe, indicate that several churches from this initial thrust took root.

On the return journey, the apostles followed the practices of the first church and developed skills and built attitude in the new congregations. The actions described in Acts 2:42–47 had been practiced in Jerusalem and passed on to Antioch; now they spread to Galatia.

Jesus had begun a mentoring system that reproduced the best beliefs and methods. The apostles passed it on to the first church, and Barnabas relayed it to Paul. In every case, the communicators had been proven, and reproduction remained consistent.

Appointing Leaders. Following the line of authority that went from Christ, through the apostles, Paul and Barnabas commissioned leaders in the new churches: "Paul and Barnabas appointed elders for them in each church and, with prayer and fasting, committed them to the Lord in whom they had put their trust" (Acts 14:23, 24). The elders at Iconium served with the authority of Christ and the blessing of the apostles; they were accountable to Paul, to Antioch, and to Jerusalem.

Not only did the apostles' prayer and fasting make a spiritual difference, these actions were symbolic for the local congregation. The laying on of hands and setting apart of elders communicated God's blessing on the leaders of the congregation. Their authority was God's, and leadership would be an absolute need if the church was to survive.

We do not know how the two men selected leaders in such a short time. During the one-year trip, they returned through five cities (they did not go back to Cyprus). Though we have no evidence that they spent an equal time in each place, we may safely assume they spent a minimum of six weeks in every city. During that time Paul and Barnabas could observe leadership ability, to get a sense of whom the congregations respected and naturally followed. They prayed and fasted for an extended period before making the final decisions. As apostles, I believe God also gave them a greater measure of discernment.

First Timothy 3 and Titus 1 make it clear that a body of belief about leadership qualifications did exist, and while the pastoral Epistles were not yet written, I believe the two apostles used the empirical data found there.

Instead of following the biblical example and having the best-qualified leaders chose other leaders, some of today's evangelical churches do it backward. They charge a nominating committee with placing names on the ballot for selection of leaders. Though I do not wish to trash congregationalism, when the group that selects the potential leaders are not properly qualified, trouble easily ensues. Typically the church chooses names from the floor of the annual business meeting; the only qualification becomes a single person's opinion. Without discussion, names are voted on.

This has nothing to do with the example of Scripture, which shows us that leaders select other leaders, based upon objective criteria. Such a system greatly reduces the chances of favoritism, subjectivism, and political infighting, which create poor choices.

The congregation can still confirm recommendations by means of a vote; it can still have the last word. But recognize that those most qualified to choose are those most qualified to lead.

A THREAT TO THE NEW CHURCHES

The first thrust into Gentile territory had proved a rousing success. After widely preaching the Gospel, Paul and Barnabas had established five to ten churches. The church at Antioch praised them for their work. It was good to be home again, but mission always creates change, and the cause of every problem is change.

Paul and Barnabas had been hounded, beaten, and conspired against during their journey, primarily by Jewish leaders who considered the Gospel blasphemy and a serious threat to their own faith. Ending the journey did not end all conflict. Determined, strategic, and smart opposition followed them home. Some men came from Judea and started teaching members of the Antioch church that they had to be circumcised and keep the law (Acts 15:1).

Paul blew his top, and a passionate debate ensued. This debate, along with the confrontation of Peter recorded in Galatians 2:1–21, indicates that there are things worth fighting for. A fighting spirit does not please God, and the anger of man does not accomplish the righteousness of God (James 1:19, 20), but there is anger that is not sin (Ephesians 4:26), and Paul channeled the energy of his anger toward a solution.

After the smoke cleared, the Antioch elders dispatched Paul and Barnabas to Jerusalem. This serious threat to the church could destroy unity and dilute the church's power. The leaders at Antioch considered it an issue for the apostles and elders who peacefully coexisted at the first church.

Remember, the converted Pharisees would find it difficult to let go of their life-style and history. The Pharisees' original purpose had been to protect the law. They had many good points: They were dedicated national heroes, accepted the Scriptures as God given, were very careful students, kept the ceremonial laws, were fervent evangelists, were sacrificing tithers, and anticipated the Messiah.[3] Six thousand Pharisees lived in Jerusalem, and many had accepted Christ as Messiah. In many of the 480 synagogues that dotted the countryside, Christ was preached.[4]

Much like the Christian legalists today, the converted Pharisees tried to keep a foot in each world. They planned strategically, forwarding their case in tightly reasoned arguments; they were excellent debaters. Their success may be reflected in the fact that twenty-five years later the writer of Hebrews rebuked and exhorted the Jerusalem church concerning the same issues (Hebrews 5:11—6:4).

At Jerusalem, the Pharisees presented their case, followed by Peter and then Paul and Barnabas. Peter asked, "Now then, why do you try to test God by putting on the necks of the disciples a yoke that neither we nor our fathers have been able to bear? No! We believe it is through the

grace of our Lord Jesus that we are saved, just as they are"
(Acts 15:10, 11).

James spoke the apostles' decision, using Scripture to
draw the conclusion, yet presenting a compromise. The apostles didn't want to place an unnecessary burden on the Gentiles, but they should ". . . abstain from food polluted by idols,
from sexual immorality, from the meat of strangled animals
and from blood" (Acts 15:20). They simply asked the Gentiles to avoid the most offensive practices. Now civil community could exist between the two groups.

Jerusalem chose some of their own men to carry the
apostles' letter to Antioch. Didn't they trust Paul and Barnabas? Of course they did, but they wanted to make a major
impression by sending fresh men into the situation. The new
men would have greater authority to confirm Paul and Barnabas's words. "We have heard that some went out from us
without our authorization and disturbed you, troubling your
minds by what they said. . . . We are sending Judas and Silas
to confirm by word of mouth what we are writing" (Acts
15:24, 27).

When the messengers arrived at Antioch, they called the
entire church together and went over the letter. Silas and
Judas remained long enough to encourage the believers and
went on their way.

How carefully the apostles had handled the threat. First
they heard everyone's argument. They made an executive
decision that all knew they had the authority to make. Further, they sent envoys to give their letter the human touch
and to make sure the false teachers in Antioch could not
accuse Paul and Barnabas of putting their own spin on the
decision. The fact that a man of Paul's brilliance and communication skills needed apostolic backup reveals how intense and powerful these enemies of the Gospel were.

As William Blake said, "Execution is the chariot of genius." Go to school on the first church's execution of this
decision. Humanize decisions, especially the controversial
ones. A good decision made by the right person can fail, if
not executed properly.

8
The Maturing Mission Church Follows Jesus

The first journey began the "Come and see" activity in the mission church, exposing people to the message, gathering them to learn about Christ, and organizing them into churches. In the second journey, initial penetration of the Gospel message occurred in cities such as Philippi, Thessalonica, and Berea. But the apostle Paul added the developmental and corrective stage of church maturation to the already-established congregations. In "Come and follow me," people began to receive training in ministry skills and the corrective visits of the apostle.

TIES THAT DON'T BIND AND GIFTS THAT DON'T MIX

Reporting to Antioch, adjusting to the role of Gentiles in the church, communicating the apostolic decree, and teaching at Antioch consumed about a year of Paul and Barnabas's ministry. Most chronologies have them returning to Antioch in about A.D. 48 and leaving on a second journey in late A.D. 49 or early A.D. 50.[1] Paul had suggested to Barnabas that they return to the Galatian region and see how the churches were doing; they would make a third swing through the region.

The two apostles were good friends. Barnabas had saved Paul's reputation and served as a communication bridge between him and the twelve. He had taken Paul under his wing and used him in developing the church at Antioch. For two years they lived together on the road, with all the familiarity that included.

But when they sat down to plan the next trip, the two men had an argument. Luke describes it as a "sharp disagreement" (Acts 15:39). The Greek word, *paroxusmos*, also means "provocation" or "quarrel."

The discord centered around the young man John Mark, who had accompanied them on their first journey. Partway through, John Mark had dropped out, and Paul did not want to bring him on the next journey. Barnabas, the "son of encouragement" wanted to continue John Mark's training. He deserved another chance and could become valuable in the Lord's service, Barnabas contended.

Many ask, "How can this be? Can two men filled with the Holy Spirit disagree? If one sinned, was it Paul or Barnabas?"

This is not a matter of spirituality or morality, but a difference in gifts. Though very evangelistic, the encourager Barnabas saw people before he saw tasks. He could encourage them into greater service for Christ, and God had called him to do that.

Paul was a driven personality. In his pre-Christian days he exhibited an unparalleled pursuit of the Pharisaic lifestyle and unremittingly determined to destroy the church. Whatever he did, Paul knew nothing of compromise or dilution: He was like a concentrated solution before you add water.

Through his lens on the world, Paul could see no virtue in slowing down or backing off. If someone quits or drops out, leave him; he had his chance, and plenty out there want it more. Paul focused on the task and saw people as instruments to accomplish the task. God had "wired" him to be task oriented.

As a result of their gift differences, Paul and Barnabas parted ways. Barnabas took John Mark and returned to Cyprus. Paul took Silas and returned to the new churches that needed more development. Both remained faithful to their callings and gifts, both were commended by the brothers, and could return with heads held high.

Many painful separations in ministry look bad at first but later reveal God's fingerprints. Though this is the last we hear of Barnabas, we hear a great deal more about John Mark. Each apostle had a great commitment to apprenticeship and chose his type of man, but Paul in particular masterfully chose, trained, and deployed apprentices.

God multiplied His church through persecution. Now He does it through differences in gifts. We may not immediately recognize the good in disagreements. They can be very painful, as this one must have been for Paul and Barnabas. As their emotions played havoc with their minds, no doubt these men questioned their decision.

Allow for gift differences in your leadership team. When you discuss plans or tasks, you will notice people have different processing grids. Perhaps when you suggest a stronger emphasis on community life, another caring but differently wired leader will argue that evangelism is the greater need. People need to come to Christ, but you might retort that you don't want healthy chicks under dead hens: The church must be warm, healthy, and loving before it can develop new converts. The two of you could argue for hours, while you both believe in evangelism. One sees the caring issue first, while the other focuses on evangelism—and it all comes down to your giftedness.

In the majority of cases, God does not want people to

part company. That should remain a last resort, only taken when feelings run so high and the viewpoints become so different that nothing else will do. In most cases, both interests should be worked on, and each man should focus his gifts. On the elder level, very little success—in fact none—occurs when men are asked to lead a ministry for which they are not passionate and gifted. Passion and gifts should, most often, match. Discover the passion and gifts in leaders during the training years that precede spiritual leadership.

STRENGTHENING THE CHURCH

After the break with Barnabas, Paul took Silas and returned to the Galatian churches. In this third visit, he sought to build up the church. Acts 15:41 and 16:5 describe his actions as strengthening, which means "making firm." Paul's intention had real results: "So the churches were strengthened in the faith and grew daily in numbers" (16:5).

Along with the Jerusalem council's decision, Paul passed on the priorities and practices of the first church. Luke structures his sentences to show cause and effect. Through the return visits, the teaching, community life, praise and outreach to the unchurched, the faith grew, people were converted, and the churches expanded.

Interestingly, in this visit Luke never records conflict with the authorities or religious establishment. Perhaps Paul had no serious encounters, or Luke did not record them. More probably, Paul engaged in no public preaching. Not that evangelism became less important for the established church—Luke dispels this idea with the comment that Paul's strengthening directly led to the church's growth. Transfer growth didn't exist in Galatia, so that meant conversion.

Paul had immediately gone to the church, so he had no opportunity to debate with the synagogue leaders or ruling authorities. Second, the church was doing quite well, thank you, at reaching others. Paul simply joined in on the fun.

The existence of eight churches made this mission less eventful in respect to open conflict.

Development and Correction

Ancient travel was slow, and Paul, Silas, and others with them stayed in each church city for some time, to minister. What Luke describes in a paragraph could have taken a year.

Strengthening the church takes intentional time and effort. This is why I believe leaders should install discipling at the very heart of the church. Paul did not return to Galatia to take up housekeeping chores or increase his power and ownership. His only interest was improving the spiritual condition of the community of Christ. Leadership means helping people work through and face resistance to their personal development. Paul led the Galatians to a new level of spiritual life by asking them to exercise their faith and do the difficult. As a result, the church increased in strength and grew daily.

Contemporary leaders face the same need to call for intentional congregational development. Leaders are charged with providing vision and vehicles—a vision cut from spiritual cloth and vehicles to carry both the hurting and healthy to maturity.

This will not come by wishing it to happen or by trying to please everyone and fit all ideologies. It calls for strategic planning and determined follow-through. On the face of things Paul's motive was to return to the churches and see how they were doing. But don't miss his prime motive: helping them move on to the next level. They needed development and correction.

The Galatian churches faced the same human problems we see in the contemporary church. Elders failed, relationships soured, believers grew disillusioned or fell away. Gossip, bitterness, serious legalism problems, and disagreements on how to handle the disobedient existed. One needs only read the Epistle to the Galatians to know this. Paul developed the church by correcting such mistakes and abuses. He would reteach the basics, address each issue, and lead them to re-establish proven priorities and practices.

Because the church needed more monitoring than Paul could give it, decentralization of ministry and leadership became crucial to church health and world mission. He had to push out the edges of world mission.

Apprenticeship Begins

Paul, an apostle with a unique call from God, had served an apprenticeship under Barnabas. Even the greats need help, especially in areas of nongiftedness. Barnabas had provided that. Now that they had parted company, Paul would begin his own apprenticing process. Without it, the apostle could not remain faithful to his call: He would have no staff to help churches and evangelize the world. Training others for ministry is the greatest investment any leader makes.

Paul chose Silas and added Timothy to their mission, after he had spent time with Timothy in Lystra. Luke characterizes Paul's travels as a group experience: "Paul and his companions" (16:6). Silas and Timothy warrant Luke's use of the plural. My educated guess is that the group held more than the duo named. Several months had passed since they left Antioch. If we know anything about Paul's desire to train others and his eye for local talent, we can imagine he allowed other less notables to tag along. It is well established that at times Paul had thirty or more traveling with him.

In Timothy we see apprenticeship in microcosm. He is a natural model for all others who aspire to follow Christ and make a difference. Luke describes him: ". . . A disciple named Timothy . . . , whose mother was a Jewess and a believer, but whose father was a Greek. The brothers at Lystra and Iconium spoke well of him" (Acts 16:1, 2).

Paul sought eager young men to join his band and be trained for ministry. However, he didn't take them sight unseen. He knew Timothy's family, their religious heritage, and his reputation among the churches. Without question Timothy stood out among the young men; otherwise Paul would have had no reason to consider him. During his previous visits to Lystra, Paul would have become acquainted with young Timothy.

I am sure Timothy wanted to go with Paul. In fact, in his first letter to the younger man, Paul identifies desire as an important element in leadership selection (1 Timothy 3:1). Timothy had proved faithful in many local matters, so he enjoyed a good reputation among the brothers. His heart was eager, and he desired training and growth. His family background included instruction in the Scriptures (2 Timothy 3:14, 15). He was willing to undergo any rite of passage his mentor required, as proved by his willingness to be circumcised, to make himself acceptable among the Jewish population.

Timothy's acceptance of this painful rite is the fruit of his commitment. All apprenticeship should require a committed action of some sort, because it will help avoid a multitude of mistakes and heartbreaks later. Though Timothy's case seems extreme by present standards, it was appropriate to the circumstances.

The apprentice will not appreciate what costs him nothing. He should at least sign an agreement as to what he will do. He should receive assignments that establish his faithfulness in the new relationship. As responsibility grows, so should commitment: The greater the responsibility, the greater the cost.

Signing contracts is a way of life; it's our culture's way of making commitments. So have ushers, teachers of every kind, facilities personnel, musicians, and so on, learn the value of faithfulness by making mini covenants to their work. Paul wrote Timothy to only turn over responsibility to "faithful men who will be able to teach others also" (2 Timothy 2:2 RSV).

Anyone chosen for training should have the qualities of Timothy. His selection teaches simple lessons about the need for apprenticeship and rites of passage. Ignore these concepts, and you will pay dearly.

MIDCOURSE CORRECTION

Regardless of how adeptly one prepares them, inevitably plans need adjusting. Even those born of God's Spirit are not perfect, because the Spirit must work through human personality.

Paul was called to take the Gospel to the Gentiles without ignoring the Jews. He never turned from his mission or was wrong in his pursuit of it. However, his own calculation and God's interventions revealed the actual geographical details. Let us remember and distinguish that God calls people to specific tasks: the pastorate, the business world, the home, or an itinerant life.

We can know general calling with certainty. For example, God has called me to teach the Scriptures and build his church. Where I live and how long I remain in a geographical location are details I attempt to calculate—but often I make a mistake. God's plan's details for our lives are found on the path of obedience; they are revealed to the obedient in time for corrective action to be taken.

Paul planned to preach in the province of Asia, but the Spirit of Jesus turned him away for a northward thrust into Bithynia. He could have turned homeward, an unacceptable choice, or could have moved northwest to the coastal city of Troas. In Troas Paul had his famous vision, in which a man from Macedonia begged him to come and preach the Gospel. In typical Pauline style, Paul and Silas didn't ask questions, they immediately departed for Macedonia.

I am not sure why evangelicals experience so much angst over God's will: It always seems clearly communicated when needed. So many Christians want to know too much too soon; they would rather walk by sight, knowing what is going to take place beforehand. However, God requires us to walk by faith, not knowing the unnecessary. Part of resting in Christ and finding His contentment involves the willingness to live in a fog over future details.

God makes a lot of midcourse corrections in our lives.

With Paul, we must obey the general thrust of His calling and allow Him to reveal the details as we go. Any other modus operandi will fail.

CONTINUING FORMATIVE ACTIVITY

Emerging from the significant developmental and corrective ministry among the Galatians, Paul and company switched gears and returned to the evangelistic phase of discipling. They entered fertile, untilled territory that brought more trouble, but more converts and churches as well. In the year he preached from Philippi to Corinth, Paul experienced every emotion, trial, and victory a herald of the Good News could know.

In Philippi and Athens. Paul had not changed the strategy: Go where the people are and preach to them. In Philippi and Athens, that meant bypassing the synagogue strategy. At Philippi, they did nothing Luke considered noteworthy until the first sabbath. Paul, Luke, Silas, Timothy, and the others went to a place of prayer and preached to the women gathered there. The Lord opened the heart of Lydia, a dealer in purple cloth from the city of Thyatira. She believed and was baptized, along with her family.

The function is to reach people with the message; the form is to use whatever is best, within the confines of integrity. Where is the spiritual interest of the city? Where do you find the most fertile ground? Paul and his apprentices got what they wanted, a convert and her network. Lydia's extended family would provide a natural means through which they could continue to preach in Philippi.

They moved on through Thessalonica and Berea, to Athens, which represents a unique experience in Paul's ministry. He was without Silas and Timothy and deeply disturbed by the idolatry. The apostle began by preaching in the synagogue and marketplace and subsequently was invited to Mars Hill, the home of new ideas. In his preaching there, he beautifully contextualized the message, as only an educated man could. Though the Athenians entertained his ideas, they finally rejected them as nonsense. Some did believe and followed him, but overall the results seemed disappointing.

Unlike the first journey, in the second Paul encountered a variety of cultures and understandings about God. This mission demonstrated Paul's versatility: He adapted his message to the culture and context without dilution or compromise. Paul showed an ability to transliterate the language of Judaism into something relevant to the Greek philosophical grid.

Though stubbornly slow about it, contemporary Christians are getting better about this. Christians use an entire church language the unchurched do not understand. Many words are a detriment to understanding: *saved, glory! grace, the Word of God, hallelujah,* and *praise the Lord* do not communicate to the non-Christian. If we want to use these terms and phrases among one another, fine, but they fuzz the issue for seekers.

Another set of terms, comprised of great biblical words, flow from our pulpits and do not communicate: *regeneration, sanctification, imputation, fellowship, justification, glorification, obedience, evangelism, witness,* and so on, mean little to the non-Christian. I do not advocate throwing them out, but they should be explained to Christians and replaced by other words that will help them reach the unchurched.

Are we willing, like Paul, to adapt our words to say the same thing, so people will fully comprehend our message? Paul's presentation on Mars Hill is radically different from anything recorded elsewhere. His example exhorts us to get with it and communicate with our generation. There is nothing wrong with moving to meet people's real spiritual needs by entering the door of felt need. A sermon series on dealing with stress, hard-to-parent teens, financial principles, or marital conflict may capture people for Christ. We can still preach expository sermons, faithful to the Scriptures, in terms people can easily relate to.

The evangelical church needs to make great changes in its "Come and see" ministry. Many churches begin outreach with whistles and horns: They do brochures, run ads in local papers, start door-to-door campaigns, and make special efforts to welcome visitors. After eighteen to twenty-four months of this, the church has enough people to be a real church, and it can pay the bills. The focus turns to "Come and follow Me" issues. This is normal and necessary, but not at the expense of "Come and see" work. When the focus turns inward, entry ports start closing, and the church retreats into unholy huddles and forgets the unreached. All phases of church life must be maintained, improved, and receive constant attention.

We cannot continue to pound out the Sunday-morning, Sunday-evening, Wednesday-night routine and expect to reach people. The more we ask people to come and sit and listen to us talk, the greater the disservice we do to them and Christ's commands. We must mobilize the saints into teams of committed believers willing to utilize their normal social groupings to pull people into the loving environment of the community of Christ. Some sit-and-listen meetings are necessary. The church should have at least one weekly gathering for praise, celebration, and motivational instruction. Our society is geared for that to take place Sunday morning. But liberate church members from other, unnecessary sit-and-listen meetings. We need to scrape away the traditional turn-offs and barnacles on the church.

Clearly, Paul took what God gave him. He had a preference for the synagogue and the Jew, but if he had to venture down to a river to talk to praying women or up to Mars Hill to debate pagan philosophers, he was game. As he exhorted Timothy: "Preach the Word . . . when it is convenient and when it is not" (2 Timothy 4:2 TLB).

Paul never had an "excuse me" ministry. All environmental conditions did not have to be copacetic. Unlike present-day evangelical churches, he never allowed believers to wait for optimum conditions before they did what was

right. Too many pastors excuse themselves on the basis of
their lack of training, outreach, or church growth: "This is a
cut-flower society." "A certain denomination has a strong-
hold here." "We are waiting for conditions to improve before
we ask this much of the congregation." "This church has
been through a lot. They need to heal before they can minister."

Hogwash! Paul would have none of this fatalistic tripe,
and neither should we. Go where people are and preach to
them. Don't let anyone talk you out of it; don't make excuses.
Get going!

In Thessalonica, Berea, and Corinth. When Paul went to the
synagogue, he reasoned with the Jews from Scripture and
debated by explaining and proving that Christ had to suffer
and rise from the dead. Such teaching evangelism required
great skill and learning. This contextualization took what
they revered and understood, the Old Testament, and made
it speak to the Gospel.

In Thessalonica, a large number believed. In Berea they
responded with great eagerness and daily examined the
Scriptures, to verify Paul's teachings. In Corinth he reasoned
on a regular basis but faced much opposition. Berea was the
most responsive; Thessalonica gave some opposition; and
Corinth responded least and provided the most opposition.

FACING THE OPPOSITION

Over the course of the six years that made up the first
and second missions, Paul and company preached in at least
fifteen cities and started a minimum of nine churches. Whenever they made an inaugural thrust, almost without excep-
tion they received opposition. Each city presented the
apostolic band with a special brand of difficulty.

Philippi: Opposition Based on a Financial Threat. In Philippi a demonically possessed slave girl followed Paul. Some

upstanding city fathers, who made a nice profit from her, owned the girl. When Paul rebuked the spirit, their handy profit left with the spirit, so the owners saw that Paul and Silas were flogged and thrown into prison.

We see a stark contrast between the early church and today's church when it comes to responding to difficulty. Modern evangelicals have been bludgeoned by secular man with the stick of suffering. "Why does a loving God allow suffering and evil?" Because they hate this question, Christians feel intimidated. The first church and mission church welcomed the question and responded so well that people were taken by the church's responses rather than their own question.

In prison, Paul and Silas sang at midnight, keeping the other prisoners awake. God sent an earthquake, but when the two men could have gone, they didn't. Instead they introduced the petrified jailer and his household to Christ and returned to their cell. Once the officials heard the stories and found that they had imprisoned Roman citizens, they wanted to let the men go. Paul and Silas played it out, insisting on an apology and a public dismissal. Their response made it possible for new believers in Philippi to hold their heads high.

Paul and Silas model the ability to make the best of a situation on the foundation of a good attitude. They were thankful, positive, and ready to preach.

Thessalonica, Berea, and Corinth: Opposition Based on a Threat to the Religious Establishment. In Thessalonica the Jewish leaders used unsavory characters to incite a mob. In Berea the agitating Thessalonian Jews pushed the apostles out of town. In Corinth the Jews so violently opposed Paul that he wrote them off and moved into a private home, to instruct those with teachable spirits. What can we glean from the synagogue opposition?

Most opposition is not birthed from ideology. Satan uses more primal needs to thwart God's plan. When an institution or individual's source of security becomes threatened, a fight ensues. Paul threatened the Philippian businessmen's income when he cast out the demon. When their members began to follow Christ, through Paul, the synagogue leaders saw the threat to their status and security. Money, ego, security, and status move man's soul.

In today's church opposition comes largely from within for two reasons. First, Satan has done such a good job of infiltrating the church that he can keep most of God's workers in committee meetings. He would much rather see a committee on evangelism than evangelism itself. Second, since the church has become so sluggish, it doesn't encounter much outside opposition. When it effectively penetrates its culture, the church will experience both a great harvest and much outside opposition.

Opponents of the Great Commission remain unaware that they stand in the way of progress. Many of their motives appear in the Jewish leadership. Both protect a way of life and want to make sure change takes place slowly, so nothing too radical happens. They oppose new ideas that might threaten existing leadership structure, require a change in financial strategy, or take the church into the dangerous territory of walking by faith.

Don't let such primal opposition shock you. Paul and Silas wasted no time shaking their heads and wringing their hands over man's subliminal motives. They knew that man's heart was evil and hard to understand and that others would oppose their efforts. Instead of lamenting and looking back, they simply thanked God for the situation and took advantage of the opportunity. Like the first church, they considered opposition normal and a sign of obedience.

A Burst of Encouragement

After being abused by the Corinthian Jews, Paul felt somewhat deflated. He was forced to pronounce judgment on them and move on to the Gentiles. Even though Crispus, the synagogue leader, and many others followed Christ, the rejection hurt Paul, who loved his own and was determined to reach them first.

God knew exactly what Paul needed and spoke to him in a vision: ". . . 'Do not be afraid; keep on speaking, do not be silent. For I am with you, and no one is going to attack and harm you, because I have many people in this city' " (Acts 18:9, 10).

So many faithful teachers and communicators of God's Good News need this word. It is open season on Christian leaders. Local pastors in particular need such encouragement. Many of us have been rejected by our congregations. Though they have different reasons from the Jews who rejected Paul, it feels as bad to us as it did to Paul. In fact, the modern pastor has a worse situation. He doesn't preach as well as Chuck Swindoll, counsel like James Dobson, care for others the way Mother Teresa does, manage like Peter Drucker, and motivate like Ronald Reagan.

Most congregations would deny they expect such performance. True, individual members do not. But if you tabulate corporate expectations, they spell *impossible*. Not only that, subliminally people know that level of quality exists, and they are not experiencing it. Mass media has created an expectational anxiety among clergy and congregation alike. This change, which has occurred in the last thirty years, has transformed the local church pastorate into the most difficult job in Christianity.

The remedy is for pastors to take God's encouragement to heart. Don't turn from the task! Move ahead, God's hand is upon you. God didn't promise Paul he would never be attacked, but the attacks would not harm him. Almost immediately after that promise Paul was taken to court, but an unusual set of events led to his release. Today the attacks continue, but God protects us and makes our faithful teaching productive in His terms.

"So Paul stayed for a year and a half, teaching them the word of God" (Acts 18:11). During that time he started to focus on the third stage of development for the mission church—reproduction.

9
The Mission Church Reproduces

The first year of the second missionary journey, as Paul and company worked in the Galatian churches, they focused on "Come and follow Me." Next, moving to the untouched cities of Macedonia for a year, they turned to "Come and see" ministry. At the end of the mission Paul settled in Corinth for eighteen months, teaching, preaching, and expanding his apprenticeship activity. This was "Come and be with Me" ministry.

Like a performer who spins plates on the ends of sticks, beginning with one, two, then adding a third and fourth, the church must concentrate on many things at the same time. The performer focuses on getting plates started while he keeps the others going. Added to this, he must keep them all balanced. The discipling church's balance includes all three phases of training and brings about healthy Christians and an evangelized world.

REPRODUCTION IN LEADERSHIP

Paul began his "Come and be with Me" ministry with Silas and Timothy as he prepared leaders through whom he could reproduce. To this apprenticeship group he soon added Luke, Priscilla, Aquila, and Apollos.

In Berea Silas and Timothy had backed into their first assignment. When the Thessalonian Jews followed Paul to Berea, he had to flee to the coast, but he left Silas and Timothy behind, to work in Macedonia. They would help develop the new churches in Philippi, Thessalonica, and Berea.

On-the-job training always works best, yet few people plan their first opportunity to go out without a mentor. God had scattered the first church before they felt ready. By splitting Paul and Barnabas, He had thrown Silas and John Mark into leadership. Now, without Paul's gradual apprenticeship process, Silas and Timothy had to stretch to a new level of leadership.

In Corinth, at first Paul worked as a tentmaker for six days and taught on the sabbath. But when Silas and Timothy arrived, he devoted himself exclusively to preaching and testifying to the Jews that Jesus is the Christ. He focused on what would produce the most fruit, teaching the Scriptures and developing leaders.

Through their association with Paul, Priscilla and Aquila became close friends and effective ministers. We can see he did a good job with them, because they did a wonderful job of instructing Apollos. They mentored Apollos, who became a great teacher. Such multiplication was the fruit of Paul's discipling priorities. Had Paul spent his time differently, I doubt Priscilla and Aquila would have followed Paul to Ephesus, known how to mentor a learned man like Apollos, or seen their apprentice so mightily used by God.

Toward the end of the mission Paul visited Ephesus for the very first time and reasoned with the synagogue, but he could not stay. He had promised to return to Antioch. After setting sail for Caesarea, he greeted the first church and went back to his home church.

REPRODUCTION THROUGH THE EPISTLES

Paul made as many visits as possible to the churches and apprenticed leaders, but he also used another means of discipling the church. In Corinth he began writing letters to the Thessalonians. These two Epistles provide valuable insight into the priorities and practices that matter at the local church level.

In reading Paul's letters to the various churches, it becomes clear that he had no clear strategy of letter writing. But he *did* have an intentional strategy for expanding the church through discipling. Need dictated his writing. The Thessalonians, confused about the return of Christ, faced the problem of members who would not work. "Why bother? Jesus is coming back very soon!" These very parasitic people took advantage of the community storehouse. Paul advised such ne'er-do-wells, "If you don't work, you don't eat." But the heart of the Thessalonian letters remains spiritual growth, the Great Commission, or the discipling process.

Key Texts for Key Churches

Every church has a distinct personality. The Galatians were legalistic; the Colossians were esoteric; and the Ephesians had lost their initial spiritual vigor. The letters Paul wrote addressed the problems the church had experienced and corrective measures it could apply. For example, the Galatians needed to focus on the fruit of the Spirit, Colossae needed to consider the person of Christ, and the Ephesians needed to look at the full employment of the church.

These Epistles also possessed prescriptive key texts that set the tone and presented overarching principles tailored to each church's personality. For the Galatians it was 5:13–26; for the Colossians, 1:15–20, 28, 29; for the Ephesians, 4:11–16; for Thessalonica, in the first letter, it was 1:5–8 and its emotional anchor, 2:7–14.

Paul also provided the churches he wrote to with some key texts that present discipling ideas in concentrate (*see*

Chart 6). Though I will not exegete the texts or attempt comprehensive commentary, I can make some observations about these discipling principles, just as a tour guide points out sights of particular interest.

Chart 6
Key Pauline Discipling Texts

For Body Ministry	1 Corinthians 12–14
For Evangelistic Responsibility	2 Corinthians 5:18–20
For Inner Spiritual Conflict	Galatians 5:16–18; 2 Corinthians 10:3–5; Ephesians 6:10–16
For Change	Romans 12:1, 2; Ephesians 4:17–32
For Individual Discipling Process	1 Thessalonians 1:5–8
For Discipling Process With a Heart	1 Thessalonians 2:7–12; Colossians 1:28, 29
For Corporate Discipling Process	Ephesians 4:2–16

Reproduction Stages. In writing to the Thessalonians, Paul presents the reproductive process as it relates to relationship (1 Thessalonians 1:5–8). This process, which focuses on the individual, occurs in three stages.

1. Demonstration. "Because our gospel came to you not simply with words, but also with power, with the Holy Spirit, and with deep conviction. You know how we lived among you for your sake" (1:5).

Apprentices need to have behavior modeled before them so they can visualize the desired attitudes and behavior. Never underestimate the power of personal influence. Former Secretary of State Henry Kissinger, a man of global influence, made the tongue-in-cheek comment: "Now when I bore people at a cocktail party, they think it's their fault." Because he demonstrated knowledge and skill in diplomacy, which has averted wars, Kissinger enjoys great influence over others.

Paul claims that he, Silas, and Timothy showed the Thessalonians something different. Their actions so thoroughly proved their commitment to Christ that no one could argue about its authenticity. The impact one person has on another depends on the opportunity one has to observe the other. Everything we do teaches, and the impact of the teacher on students is the first step in the discipling process.

2. *Imitation.* "You became imitators of us . . ." (1:6). An inviting demonstration demands eager imitation. God demands that men and women imitate His disciples, but only when His disciples demonstrate an exciting, meaningful life will others want to follow.

The word translated "imitators" is a replacement word for *disciple*:

> The term "imitator" is one link between the disciples of Jesus in the Gospels and the believers of the early church. Although the word disciple [*mathetes*] is curiously absent from the epistles, Michaelis' conclusion is representative of recent scholarship: The *mathetes* . . . and the *mimetes* are one and the same.[1]

Imitator describes a fundamental part of discipling, learning from others and using them as guides. Michael Wilkins elaborates:

> It is used in texts such as (1 Corinthians 4:16; Ephesians 5:1; 1 Thessalonians 2:14; Hebrews 6:12); and *summimetes* ("fellow imitator," Philippians 3:17) are always joined in the New Testament with the verb *ginomai* ("be, become") and are thus similar in meaning to the simple verb *mimeomai* (2 Thessalonians 3:7, 9; Hebrews 13:7; 3 John 11).[2]

> The New Testament calls on believers to imitate other believers, Christ, and God. Human objects are

those most numerously given for imitation. Human imitation ranges from simple comparison with the conduct of other believers (1 Thessalonians 2:14) to presentation of examples of conduct to imitate (Philippians 3:17; 2 Thessalonians 3:7, 9; Hebrews 6:12; 13:7). Paul gives himself as an example for imitation (1 Corinthians 4:16; 11:1; Philippians 3:17; 2 Thessalonians 3:7, 9), but he does not hold himself up as the ideal of mature perfection. . . . Twice Paul calls for his readers to imitate himself, but at the same time he names Christ as the final object of their imitation (1 Corinthians 11:1; 1 Thessalonians 1:6).[3]

Imitation is the sincerest form of flattery, but never confuse impersonation with imitation. Witness the modern scourge called the Elvis impersonator. In that case, impersonation means trying to be Elvis, trying to replace him. It denies the impersonator's personhood and distorts the one impersonated.

The church is not trying to make Christian clones who share the same haircuts, mannerisms, language, and clothing styles, as if they came off a Christian assembly line. Leaders need to allow for individuality and obvious differences. While impersonation tries to be someone else, imitation focuses on learning characteristics from someone else. Characteristics, not clothing, haircuts and phraseology, need to be imitated and reproduced.

The difference between impersonation and imitation becomes apparent in Paul and Timothy's relationship. You could hardly find two men more different in looks and personality. Paul was a driven man, while Timothy was timid. Paul spoke out directly and to the point, while Timothy danced around issues. Paul was a cosmopolitan scholar, while Timothy had received his education at home. While Paul thrived on conflict, Timothy got heartburn.

But though obvious differences existed, the two men had vital similarities:

Therefore I urge you to imitate me. For this reason I
am sending to you Timothy, my son whom I love, who
is faithful in the Lord. He will remind you of my way
of life in Christ Jesus, which agrees with what I teach
everywhere in every church.

1 Corinthians 4:16, 17

"I want you to imitate me," Paul writes. "And in order
for you to have a model, I will send Timothy. Why do I send
Timothy? He is just like me when it comes to the characteristics of walking with Christ." Paul demonstrated the Christ-
like characteristics, and Timothy imitated them. Because
reproduction focuses on characteristics, not personality or
appearance, Timothy could serve as a stand-in for Paul.

Later Paul wrote Timothy:

You, however, know all about my teaching, my way of
life, my purpose, faith, patience, love, endurance,
persecutions, sufferings. . . . But as for you, continue
in what you have learned and have become convinced
of, because you know those from whom you learned it.

2 Timothy 3:10, 14

Imitation of characteristics is God's plan for reproduction.

3. Reproduction. "And so you became a model to all the believers in Macedonia and Achaia. The Lord's message rang
out from you not only in Macedonia and Achaia—your faith
in God has become known everywhere" (1 Thessalonians
1:7, 8).

Wilkens comments on *tupos*, the Greek word for "model":

Related concepts are found in the use of *tupos* ["type,
example"] which occurs in several contexts with
"imitation" terms [Philippians 3:17; 1 Thessalonians
1:7; 2 Thessalonians 3:9] *hupogrammos* ("example" cf. 1

Peter 1:21), and the adverbial forms *kathos* ["just as," 2 Corinthians 1:5] and *hos* ["like," Luke 6:40].[4]

Reproduction takes place when the apprentice becomes a model. To become a model means the student has reached a point in his development where others can follow him, and they, too, will take on the characteristics of Christ. Paul mentions the apex of modeling when he says the message went out to the entire region, and the Thessalonians' faith was widely known.

Demonstration invites imitation, which leads to reproduction. When reproduction takes place in large volumes, exponential growth begins, and we call that multiplication.

Tupos means "a mark left by a blow." We're not talking here about an artist's carefully crafted clay model. It conjures up the vision of a person falling into the mud and leaving his imprint. Modeling does not mean you leave an impression you have judicially planned; it is the mark of your true person. Modeling means demonstrating the way you truly are. You cannot possibly be authentic, have contact with people, and do anything else.

THE HEART OF REPRODUCTION

Though the priorities taught in 1 Thessalonians 1:5–8 are a must for every church, the prescribed process also needs a heart. Paul describes that heart in 1 Thessalonians 2:7–14, which teaches that a healthy church requires the tenderness of a mother and the leadership of a father—in other words, leaders must have the parent hearts.

Historically proponents of discipling have overlooked the need for supportive relationships, instead viewing fellowship aspects of reproduction as a by-product. But I am convinced discipling cannot take place powerfully and productively unless the leadership and congregation at large possess a parent's heart. A church without a heart is a dysfunctional family, and discipling will not survive there.

The Tenderness of a Mother

Paul expresses this with a vivid metaphor: ". . . We were gentle among you, like a mother caring for her little children" (1 Thessalonians 2:7). A mother naturally tends to be gentle, to give and not take, and she desires her children to have it better than she did. The entertainer Cher had been raised in poverty, without enough shoes or nice clothes. When she became wealthy, she bought her daughter hundreds of pairs of shoes: It's only natural to want to do nice things for your children.

The Greek word Paul employed for "caring" means "to warm and cherish." When a child scrapes his knee or is in some sort of pain, he reaches for Mom. Her gentleness and acceptance make a hard world soft. In his mother's lap the child feels special and loved, apart from performance. A young person's life includes the rugged terrain of comparison, competition, and rejection. Pressures to conform, excel academically, take drugs, and engage in premarital sex can crush a child's moral shell and spirit. Every child needs acceptance, physical touching, and a place where he is number one. When he fails, a mother's acceptance brings healing. Her tenderness returns balance to his life.

Christians also need a place of security and safety, of gentleness and acceptance. To achieve this, everyone in the body of Christ is to care for others. However, by personality, gifts, and spirituality, some people function better as the church's emotional anchors.

Particularly after disappointment, when we feel discouraged or life has dealt us a painful blow, we need care. Sometimes even the strongest people need help. At such times, the emotional anchors notice the need first and mobilize other body members to the rescue.

Many a productive person has been lost because emotional anchors were not esteemed in a discipling environment. If everyone were like Paul, John Mark could never have helped Paul in later life. It took Barnabas to see the potential in John Mark and meet that need.

Emotional anchors make the community of Christ by far the most fertile environment for developing people to reach the world. Those who would normally have dropped out of the church during a rough time can be held by the emotional anchors. After the crisis ends, often recovered persons make a major contribution to the cause of Christ.

To effectively use the tenderness of a mother in the congregation, leaders must provide discipleship for the emotional anchors. If these Christians do not have the same values as the total body, their great ability to empathize may lead them to take an adversarial position toward church leadership. If they are not biblically sound, they may feel like championing an antiscriptural idea.

Emotional anchors also need to network needy people to other types of gifted people, to balance the scale. Without balance, discipleship abuse results. When the church enables negative behavior under the guise of "being there for somebody," empathy and support have gone out of control. On the other hand, when the task takes precedence over other needs, as a matter of course, task has gotten out of control. The church needs a balance.

The Leadership of a Father

While the church family needs the tenderness of a mother, to retain balance, it also needs the leadership of a father. The father has a more cognitive role; he is the authority figure: "For you know that we dealt with each of you as a father deals with his own children, encouraging, comforting and urging you to live lives worthy of God, who calls you . . ." (1 Thessalonians 2:11, 12).

The father relates to his children on a different level from the mother. Paul describes the mother as caring and the father as leading. Both care and lead sometimes, but their primary roles are different. Together they bring balance, giving the family two sides of love. The father sets the family course, points in a certain direction as to the kind of people family members are to become. "This is what we esteem; this is what we stand for; this is why; and this is how we are going to get there."

In the church, the elders, pastors, teachers, and other church leaders normally play the father's role. A father's love is just as important as a mother's, though it is manifested differently.

Three synonyms for love, used in 1 Thessalonians 2:11, 12, describe a father's leadership.

1. Encouraging. This word's history means "to help or to exhort to a certain pattern of conduct." This is "Come and follow Me" leadership, which says, "This is where we need to go. I will take the responsibility to train you and help you."

My youngest son owned a wonderful bike he refused to ride. I knew fear held him back from adventuring out into the streets, so one Saturday I announced we would be learning to ride the bike that day. He voiced his desire not to learn and insisted he didn't want to go. I told him I understood his feelings, but we were going anyway.

I took him across the street and held the back of the seat while he pedaled around the parking lot. Within five minutes, he was riding on his own. My son had so much fun that he rode around for several hours and didn't want to get off the bike to come in for dinner.

I made him go, and he resisted me. Was that tender? Not in the sense that we usually speak of it. Was it loving? You bet it was! I took him where he didn't want to go so he could do what he really wanted. He wanted to ride a bike, like the rest of the boys, but he needed some firm direction.

The church is filled with people who want to do right and make a difference for Christ. But they fear the changes such a commitment might bring. Fatherly leadership points in a certain direction and takes people there. Firm leadership insists on a course of action that is needed to overcome resistance. The essence of pastoring is motivating people to engage in behaviors that do not come naturally.

2. Comforting. This means "encouraging to a certain kind of behavior, but to do so by addressing feelings." *Encouraging* emphasizes the appeal to a person's logic. This word focuses on the Christian's emotional dimension.

Like any other meaningful relationship, church life has a necessary ebb and flow. Moments of great joy and excitement are followed by down times. Sometimes we must swallow hard as the color bleeds out of life, leaving only black and white.

For example, we may disagree with a new method or idea in the church community. At moments like these, the appeal to emotional equity may save the body from serious trouble. One person I dealt with stood against a particular methodology required of a large number of people. He gave me all the reasons why he did not agree with the methods. After several hours of discussion, I asked him for a personal favor. "Would you please go along in order to keep peace in the body? We don't want our unity destroyed over this. I may be wrong; you may be wrong; but the greater good is that the majority of the people support the action." This man went along because he knew sometime he would desire others to follow a course of action he supported. My appeal to the emotional side made the difference.

3. Urging. This means "to summon to court." Family life has absolutes that the father must urge all members to follow. To a child, he issues decrees such as, "You will practice the trumpet," "You will do your homework," "You will follow these moral standards of our family." He provides leadership and takes people through hard experiences. Because of leadership, soldiers will charge an enemy fortress, when they know that most of them will perish. The father can lead the family, because he believes in the cause and has enough emotional equity built up to support the action.

The Heart of a Parent

Combine the tenderness of the mother and the leadership of the father, and you get the heart of a parent.

When my wife and I attended a meeting for parents of

teenagers, I was most struck by the depth of feeling that filled the room. One couple had driven all night just to discuss their daughter's behavior. That room held hope, pain, tears of joy, anxiety concerning the future, despair, and frustration, along with total emotional investment on the part of every parent. I couldn't tell if we were bad, great, or normal parents.

One thing came across clearly, though: parents' hearts go out to a child. They would willingly rip out their hearts and put them on a platter for a son or daughter. God gives mothers and fathers an enlarged capacity to accept their children; one of life's great glories is the ability of parents to forgive a child who has hurt them deeply.

A church that grows people has the heart of a parent and experiences all the emotions of the parents in that room. The combined roles of father and mother provide a model for the community of Christ. When a wife submits to her husband's authority, the children find it easier to submit to the father's wishes. If the wife honors her husband, and the husband loves the wife as Christ loves the church, children are more likely to do the same. When the tenderness of a mother (the emotional anchor) and the leadership of the father (the authority and directional anchor of the home) work together, more often than not they develop healthy, responsible children. Children need both feminine and masculine qualities.

The Combined Parental Roles in the Church

When parents accept their respective roles and each other, the home can become a powerful instrument for good. I don't insist that my wife think the same way I do or enjoy the activities I do. I don't think she is less of a person because she doesn't care for sports, nor does she think less of me because I don't enjoy gardening. We work well together because we accept each other and function in our roles.

Likewise the body of Christ has different gifts. Full employment of these gifts means everyone shares in creating the community environment (1 Corinthians 12—14; Ephesians 4:16; 1 Peter 4:10). We embrace one another; we don't shoot anyone because he is more or less than others.

Strong leaders often look at those not gifted in leadership and consider them less important to the cause. On the other hand, emotional anchors often consider their leaders unfeeling and only interested in getting a job done. In contemporary evangelicalism I see a tendency to focus on a person's nongiftedness and label it weakness. Rather than thanking God for another's gifts, people expect him to excel in his nongifted areas.

The way a congregation views its pastor accentuates this. Most congregations claim to believe in spiritual gifts and the concept of acceptance of others in the body. First Corinthians 12—14 simply teaches that a hand cannot say to a foot, "Because you are not a hand, you are less a part of the body." In other words, "Because you don't excel in the same area I do, you are less valuable or less spiritual than I am." I also cannot say, "I don't need you," because God says I do need other members of the body.

People will accept one another's strengths and weaknesses, but they do not extend the same courtesy to the clergy. They look at a pastor's strengths, and instead of thanking God for his gifts and allowing him to concentrate on those areas, they roundly criticize his nongiftedness and hound him to work on his "weakness." Few people could survive the ridiculous expectations churches place on their leaders. We stand them up in front and proceed to pick them apart.

You might think I am overreacting, but if you talked to the number of pastors I do and heard about their hurts, you would not accuse me of that. These men hurt primarily because of the accusations of perfectionists and an unaccepting church populace. The cream of the crop in talent overcome such opinions by sheer power of personality and gifts; the church will accept someone if he is talented enough, overlooking his nongifted areas. Tragically, we do not give the same grace to the less gifted.

The exhortation to accept the giftedness of others also cuts into the value we place on nonprofessional ministry. If you spend time in the hospital and several congregational members visit you, but the pastor does not, do you feel left out? Later, at the coffee klatch, you may sound off about how you were never visited in the hospital. If you really believe this, do you realize you rank your pastor's visit above your friends'? What are you saying about your friends?

I challenge anyone to find a scriptural rationale for saying that the love-gifted emotional anchors who visited you didn't count. The pastor has the job of mobilizing ministry. He might engage in visitation, but he can do his job better if others take it on.

It is imperative that we invite the entire congregation up to the same level of ministry as the clergy. We must restore the ordinary believer's dignity. Either the average church member's work is as important as the clergy's, as Scripture reports, or it is not; we can't have it both ways. If the congregation's ministry is not important, we must dismiss it from any meaningful responsibility. But the denial of the spirit of 1 Corinthians 12—14 destroys any opportunity for the heart of a parent to excel churchwide.

The heart of a parent is the corporate glue that holds the church together: We need the tenderness, the exhortation, and the leadership. It will never happen if we expect that only from one person or two or ten. A parent's heart only develops when we embrace the entire body, the corporate culture. We need to stop pointing the finger at the weaknesses of our fellow Christians and start embracing the roles we are to play and the gifts God has given.

Part IV

THE DISCIPLING CHURCH

If a New Testament model for the discipling church exists, we see it at Ephesus, a church Paul founded and pastored for three years. I believe Paul's convictions and strategy reached their apex here and that the Ephesian church provides the contemporary congregation with the best scriptural model.

The discipling church adds "Come with Me" to the other stages. Here reproduction takes place on a churchwide scale. Paul develops a team of apprentices, many of whom are ready to do ministry on their own, apart from Paul's daily influence. The individuals, well trained in Paul's methods, were ready to step out and cause the congregation as a whole to reproduce.

To appreciate what went on in Ephesus, we will look at the congregation, its pastoral goals, and the leaders who brought it to multiplication.

10
Ephesus: The Congregation and Its Priorities

In the grasp of a Spirit-engendered wanderlust, a few months after he arrived in Antioch Paul again set off for Galatia. What did he do on his fourth visit? No surprise: "... Paul set out from there and traveled from place to place throughout the region of Galatia and Phrygia, strengthening all the disciples" (Acts 18:23). Then he made a swing south, inland to Ephesus.

There Paul found a group of twelve "tweeners," who straddled the theological chasm between the Old and New Covenants (Acts 19:1–7). Familiar with the message of John the Baptist, they had repented, experienced the baptism for repentance, and had believed in Jesus. However, they had not received the Holy Spirit or experienced His manifestations. Paul proceeded to baptize them, and after the laying on of hands, they spoke in tongues and prophesied.

THE EPHESIAN CHURCH

Paul decided to reinstitute the synagogue strategy. Toward the end of the second journey he had been briefly but well received in Ephesus, so now he returned to fertile soil.

For three months he argued persuasively, stirring up the obligatory opposition. The enemy used the usual weapons of obstinate attitudes and slander to get Paul thrown into the street; it was the best thing that could have happened. Remember, go where the people are and preach to them. Paul went to the hall of Tyrannus and lectured daily for two years. During that time, the entire province of Asia heard the word of the Lord.

Luke impressively links the school to evangelism with the expression "so that." Whatever Paul said in those three- to four-hour lectures he gave in the heat of the day had a profound effect on his students.[1] The local ministry proved powerful as well: "God did extraordinary miracles through Paul" (Acts 19:11). God's people exercised power over evil spirits and ". . . the name of the Lord Jesus was held in high honor. Many of those who believed now came and openly confessed their evil deeds. . . . In this way the word of the Lord spread widely and grew in power" (Acts 19:17, 18, 20).

Locally and throughout all Asia, the Ephesian church became mighty. Because it represents the best of what it means to be a discipling church, God has left us with a great deal of information about this congregation. Paul spent three years as its founding pastor; he wrote a letter to the Ephesian church and wrote his pastoral letters to Timothy while the younger man led the Ephesian church. The churches mentioned in Revelation 2, 3 are some Paul planted during his ministry at Ephesus.

Putting together the information we have about Ephesus, I have established three keys to the discipling church:

1. *The priorities of the people or congregation.* Paul's letter to Ephesus, written only a few years after he left, describes the church's personality and priorities. Through this we

can identify what it means to become part of a discipling congregation.

2. *The pastoral priorities.* What does it mean to lead a congregation that disciples? Paul's letters to Timothy describe the role a pastor plays in making the church a discipling one. The apostle identifies priorities and practices that must be part of Timothy's leadership.

3. *The leadership community and outreach.* Paul's lectures in the hall of Tyrannus served as a training ground for new leaders and a place in which evangelism could occur. By piecing together the relationship between training and evangelism and seeing how it was done locally and in Asia, we can discover Ephesus's formal strategies for reproduction and multiplication.

How did Paul use these to build the church that best shows us how to disciple today? He began with a method we have already studied: He went where the people were.

Building the Congregation

To build a church, Paul had to allow the Gospel to take root in the Ephesian community. After all, if it doesn't work for the ordinary man in the street, why go on? For three months he employed the Scriptures in evangelistic teaching and debate in the synagogue; then he took a believing core into the streets for evangelism and into the lecture hall for instruction. God worked in a mighty way, performing signs and wonders.

Using ordinary people, Paul built his ministry on the "nuts and bolts" work. The proof for any ministry is the answer to the question "Does it work in the marketplace?" Are the power and reality of God present? Are new people converted, taught, and reproduced? Paul planted a powerful ministry in Ephesus, and Luke describes its influence: ". . . The name of the Lord Jesus was held in high honor. Many of those who believed now came and openly confessed their evil deeds" (Acts 19:17, 18). Not only did they confess, these new believers demonstrated their repentance through concrete actions: "A number who had practiced sorcery brought their scrolls together and burned them publicly . . ." (Acts 19:19). Finally, "In this way the word of the Lord spread widely and grew in power" (Acts 19:20).

Fundamentally the church is not about strategy or methods, but about rescuing man from sin and populating heaven. The Great Commission provides the strategy, and discipling is the method, but if people are not reached, the church's efforts miss the point.

The local church environment forms the foundation for launching into wider ministry. So the true discipling church begins with reaching and building people, then moves on to leadership development and multiplication through church planting. Every local church should have the goal of influencing the world (Acts 1:8). To see Paul's plan for reaching this goal, we can investigate his teachings to the Ephesian church.

THE EPISTLE TO THE EPHESIANS

Paul wrote this letter from a Roman prison, in about A.D. 61. Five years had passed since he had been in Ephesus. Scholars commonly believe the apostle intended his letter for all the churches started during his Ephesian ministry, which would have included the seven identified in Revelation 2, 3 and several unnamed congregations.

Paul wrote Ephesians to the ordinary believer, presenting an overall theology for the church and its members. In the letter he reveals the priorities of the discipling church, ones remarkably similar to the teachings of Jesus, the first church, and the mission church.

Just as Paul had begun the mission to the Ephesians by scratching the Jewish mind where it itched—the identity of the Messiah, which he proved through a thorough study of the Old Testament—he entered the Ephesian Gentiles' felt need by moving into the hall of Tyrannus and a more contemporary theology. Though his ministry in Ephesus had started with the Jews, eventually the Gentiles greatly outnumbered them. Therefore Paul began to develop his own expression of theology, based of course on the truth God revealed to him. This letter represents some of Paul's very best theological explanations of God's gracious work toward mankind.

God's Purpose in Redemption (Ephesians 1:3–23). After greeting and blessing the Ephesians, Paul describes God's loving action in Christ as giving him great pleasure. Most naturally He loves others by giving of himself. Paul describes God's great purpose, saying: "And he made known to us the mystery of his will according to his good pleasure, which he purposed in Christ, to be put into effect when the times will have reached their fulfillment—to bring all things in heaven and on earth together under one head, even Christ" (vv. 9, 10). God would place all things together under the leadership of His Son.

The goal? "In order that we, who were the first to hope in Christ, might be for the praise of his glory" (1:12). In bringing all things under Christ's leadership and rescuing us from our plight, God receives the glory. The glory of God is all He is and has; it is the purpose of mankind in the redemptive plan. God gets glory when He is revealed; the only response to the revealing of His person is that mankind will give Him glory. For that reason, Paul closes the first chapter with a prayer of thanksgiving.

God's Purpose in an Individual's Life (Ephesians 2:1–22). Satan and his cohorts have a very prominent place in this letter: Paul focuses on the enemy's role in man's separation from God, the spiritual conflict he faces, and the tools needed for the conflict (2:1, 2; 6:12–18). Chapter 2 is the home of Paul's great text on God's specific action, joined to man's, that brings about spiritual birth: "For it is by grace you have been saved, through faith—and this not from yourselves, it is the gift of

God—not by works, so that no one can boast. For we are God's workmanship, created in Christ Jesus to do good works, which God prepared in advance for us to do" (2:8–10).

Chapter 1 spoke of bringing God and man together. This chapter speaks of bringing Jew and Gentile together as one in Christ (vv. 11–22).

God's Purpose in His Church (Ephesians 3:1–21). In the first two chapters Paul has beautifully set the stage for the grand sweep of God's gracious action in Christ. Now he focuses on his own purpose, personalizing the Great Commission: ". . . I, Paul, the prisoner of Christ Jesus for the sake of you Gentiles—" In the first nine verses of this chapter Paul clearly states the nature of his mission.

Ephesians 3:10–21 make a vital connection that ties these three chapters together: "His intent was that now, through the church, the manifold wisdom of God should be made known to the rulers and authorities in the heavenly realms, according to his eternal purpose which he accomplished in Christ Jesus our Lord" (3:10, 11).

In the early part of that verse, "now" reveals much. Throughout history, God has used a variety of means to reveal His manifold wisdom. Now, using the invention called the church, He reveals His wisdom in sending Christ.

This passage boosts the average believer's ego, because he knows he has an important role, and explains why Paul spent his life planting and developing churches. From it, we know why God ordained the discipling church as His vehicle for reaching the world. The church has the abilities, finances, gifts, and Spirit to get the job done. The unified, trained body of Christ is the most powerful expression of God on the face of the earth.

Therefore Paul ends in a marvelous prayer that finishes: "Now to him who is able to do immeasurably more than all we ask or imagine, according to his power that is at work within us, to him be glory in the church and in Christ Jesus throughout all generations, for ever and ever! Amen" (3:20, 21).

The grand, unchallenged purpose of God's gracious rescue of mankind is for His pleasure and glory. Gradually He reveals Himself by unveiling the mystery of Christ taking up residency in man's spirit and fusing all believers into a supernatural organism called the church. Revealing God's glory simply means revealing God. Now God reveals Himself through the church. "To him be the glory in the church" means God will use the church as his primary vehicle.

The first half of Paul's Ephesian letter contains the grand theology upon which all Christianity stands. It establishes Christ as the head; but the church is the body of Christ. Its arms, legs, hands, and feet—its incarnation—exists through regenerate men and women.

The second half of the letter radically applies the earlier theology. The first three chapters present a gracious, pleasurable action of God, in which He created a regenerate and chosen people for whom He has a plan. He will express His glory through them, the church. What kind of people must they be?

THE PEOPLE'S PRIORITIES

The discipling church glorifies God by producing the healthy Christians Jesus described in John 15:7–17. In the letter to the Ephesians, Paul presents the priorities of the discipling church to the average saint. The entire congregation will need to read and understand it, so Paul presents biblical truths in a contextualized manner that leaves out technical jargon meant for leaders. As the pastoral letters are meant for leadership, Ephesians is for the church populace.

Wise pastors follow Paul's example by expressing discipling principles in communication forms the congregation will appreciate. The majority of Christians find jargon and motivational teaching boring and irrelevant. Strategy, principles of creating church environment, and leadership development do not turn on most Christians. Practical teaching that helps make their lives meaningful and gives them skills for the hard times motivates them.

Putting Doctrine Into Practice

Orthopraxy (right practice) is always derived from orthodoxy (right doctrine). Those who say, "Let's not be doctrinal, let's be practical," amuse me, because I find it impossible to be practical without being doctrinal. Doctrine drives practice. Paul's applications are helpful because they grow out of a theological base.

Modern church thinkers have increasingly lost sight of this truth. Contemporary theology often allows application to grow from pragmatism and the social sciences. Rarely will a church pastor, board, or team start from a theological base, identify principles, and apply them in a contextualized form.

Paul's application of the body-of-Christ concept does that. It is genius—God's genius, that is.

Unity in Christ's Body. Paul made the theological point that God had fused Jew and Gentile into a supernatural organism called the church (2:11–22). He applies this by saying, "Make every effort to keep the unity of the Spirit through the bond of peace" (4:3). There is one Lord, one faith, and one baptism, therefore the church should be one in practice.

I have labored in divisive environments. Discipling *can* take place there, but it lives in ever-present danger. People may hang their bitterness on the hooks of principles such as the apprenticeship of leaders, philosophical purity at the leadership level, and decentralization of leadership. Those not in the discipling loop tend to use what they are not experiencing as potential combat zones; it provides them with a place to stand. Others oppose a controversial principle in order to get a reading on their power gauge. Working in a divided church is one of the hardest, saddest tasks a Christian faces.

Paul exhorts Christians to "make every effort" to keep unity because the price of division is so high. Combat within the walls of the church destroys vision, saps energy, and causes people to want to get out. But unity is sweet, as the psalmist wrote: "How good and pleasant it is when brothers live together in unity! It is like precious oil poured on the head, running down on the beard ..." (Psalm 133:1, 2). Don't let this priceless jewel slip through your fingers as a result of simple neglect, pettiness, ego gratification, or the need for immediate action.

Conversely, if you are in a divisive situation, do not wait until everything gets fixed before you start developing people. In fact, in some cases the problem can't be fixed, and you must go on or die. If people will not deal with the reason for factions, press on to the future with whoever will go. For many pastors, leading others into the future is the only and best option.

Determine to lead people in a positive action. Some will always snap at your heels, saying, "Fix this." "What about that?" "Don't you care about the issues?" and so on. Don't allow the disobedient to trivialize your work. If you wait for everyone in a hostile environment to support you, the enemy wins. As Jesus instructed the fatigued fishermen, "Launch out into the deep." You have nothing to lose, except your job. Would you rather lose your dignity before God or a job?

You can only get people's focus off the wrong by showing them enough of what is right for its magnetic pull to capture them. But honestly, many will never come along at all. Jesus cared about those who would not come along, and He died for them, but He also stopped working with them and focused on His followers.

As in the first church and the mission church, a common vision unified the discipling church. Paul goes on to explain how the Ephesians could preserve that unity.

Preserving the Disciple-Making Church Through Gifts. Traditionally, Christian leaders have seen spiritual gifts and discipling philosophy as separate topics. In fact, many discipling organizations and thinkers believe the two work against each other. One group I had part in went so far as to play down spiritual gifts and discourage its members from seeking or developing them; they explained away their paranoia by saying exercising gifts was not an evidence of spiritual maturity.

The divisive nature of the manifestational or "charismatic" gifts added to this outlook. For many years the charismatic movement focused on God's power manifested in signs and wonders; they created emotionally charged worship and little else. Spiritual gifts became a charismatic specialty, and charismatics understood and esteemed their discovery and exercise. As the movement has matured, members have developed a more moderate theology of the Holy Spirit and have started to value discipling philosophy. This move toward balance is both right and natural.

On the noncharismatic evangelical front, much paranoia has dissipated, resulting in an increased interest in spiritual gifts.

Historically, noncharismatics have focused on discipling teaching that proposes to produce a certain kind of person, characterized by personal devotion to Christ and a catalog of ministry skills. Though not intentionally, this has tended to favor an assembly-line approach to personal development. Everyone looks, talks, acts, and thinks alike; they all have the same arsenal of ministry skills.

The existence of both spiritual gifts and discipling ministry is good news for both charismatic and noncharismatic evangelism. The church cannot truly disciple without both dimensions. It needs historic discipleship's emphasis on creating a certain kind of person, but that alone creates a one-dimensional church. Emphasis on character and ministry skills are foundational, but adding spiritual-gifts development brings the body the creativity and balance that will make it a powerful tool in God's hands. The development of spiritual gifts is so vital that it became one of Paul's first applications concerning what makes a discipling church.

Spiritual tools. As a teenager I worked at a lumberyard, where I made picnic tables. The yard had every woodworking tool imaginable; with the latest technology, I could put together several picnic tables a day. If I wanted to make a picnic table at home, however, I would have found it very difficult. Without those tools, the same job would have become a long, tedious process.

In many places the church functions without all its tools. While many discipling-model churches carry out this ministry using only a few tools, God has equipped His church to do more ministry and more creative ministry. Without the full exercise of gifts, the church cannot be the full mosaic God planned. Full employment will only become reality through the use of gifts.

Paul introduces gifts by the use of the phrases "grace has been given" (4:7), "gave gifts to men" (4:8), and "it was he who gave" (4:11). Christ is ascended and has left behind supernatural tools for His church to use. In other writings Paul affirms that every believer has been given at least one supernatural tool. Three times in 1 Corinthians 12 Paul uses the phrase "each one" (or "each man") when referring to the distribution of supernatural tools. Peter confirms every believer's possession of a supernatural tool: "Each one should use whatever gift he has received to serve others, faithfully administering God's grace in its various forms" (1 Peter 4:10). Some of the gifts are for leadership, others for direct contact with those who need help. Harmonious working together of gifts is essential to an effective church (1 Corinthians 12—14).

Therefore a discipling church focuses on building a foundation of theology, as Ephesians suggests, and teaching people about their tools, to help them discover and develop their gifts. When this occurs, a wide variety of personality types, who express their commitment to Christ in a multidimensional way, populate the discipling church. Traditional word-oriented disciples, who have typically characterized disciple making, coexist with those who have nonverbal gifts that lay the groundwork for reaching people in a demonstrated service and by expressing love to the needy.

Gifted Leaders Set Discipleship Into Motion. "It was he who gave some to be apostles, some to be prophets, some to be evangelists, and some to be pastors and teachers" (4:11). God has given gifted leadership to His church, and these people have the responsibility to prepare believers to be effective ministers where they live, work, and play. The church populace should understand their relationship to leadership, know why gifted leadership exists, and how it will benefit them in their relationship to Christ.[2]

Leaders, remember why God placed you in the body. Like any other gift, leadership should be used to serve and equip the body, so that body can praise and glorify God. On a functional basis, this means practicing a commitment to disciple making so that individual Christians will be healthy and reproducing.

COMMITMENTS OF THE DISCIPLING CHURCH

To be a discipling church, a congregation must maintain its unity, discover its giftedness, and respond to its leadership. In order to reach its full expression, it must also make four major commitments identified in Ephesians 4:12–16; 5:1:

> To prepare God's people for works of service, so that the body of Christ may be built up until we all reach unity in the faith and in the knowledge of the Son of God and become mature, attaining to the whole measure of the fullness of Christ.
>
> Then we will no longer be infants, tossed back and forth by the waves, and blown here and there by every wind of teaching and by the cunning and craftiness of men in their deceitful scheming. Instead, speaking the truth in love, we will in all things grow up into him who is the Head, that is, Christ. From him the whole body, joined and held together by every supporting ligament, grows and builds itself up in love, as each part does its work. . . .
>
> Be imitators of God, therefore. . . .

A Commitment to Preparation

The word translated "prepare" in Ephesians 4:12 is *katartismon,* which can mean "to set a broken bone, mend a frayed net, furnish an empty house, or restore to mint condition." Setting a broken bone implies putting people back together again. Mending a frayed net communicates working with discouraged, tired, and burned-out people. Furnishing a house means giving them the equipment they need. Restoring to mint condition could refer to helping people get well from a variety of debilitating injuries inflicted by life. The word communicates a multidimensional restoration of God's people in order to prepare them to be ministers.

All the above activity is discipling and part of the Great Commission. Whatever helps a person become prepared to grow in Christ, learn his or her gifts, and begin to make a difference is discipling. Leadership ties all activity together and directs discipling toward a common goal. Each part of the process is intentionally guided and seen as a small part of the larger corporate plan. We counsel Joe to help him manage his problem so he can get started in a small group. The small group will take him at his own speed to a more mature walk, to the discovery of his gifts, and will provide him with guidance as to where he can employ his ability.

Congregation members have the responsibility of availing themselves of the various vehicles that will prepare them for ministry. It might mean forming or becoming part of a support group that helps others with a certain life-style or problem, such as single parenting, singleness, or unemployment. Or a member might be ready for apprenticeship and needs to make himself available for training.

When members do not give themselves to ministry preparedness, something the body needs done will go undone. Tragically, such disobedience also leads to the uninvolved person's never becoming what God wants. Spiritual maturity requires submission to spiritual authority, involvement in training and preparedness, and the accountability of working with others toward a common goal.

What Is Ministry? *Ministry* has improperly become synonymous with *the clergy*. Ministry simply means to serve, and Ephesians 4:12–16 indicates that all God's people are to do the work of service or ministry. "Ministry is what a minister does," would be a better definition. A minister may do some things normally associated with professional clergy, such as hospital visitation, baptizing, and so on, but ministry means much more. It means being trained to exercise your gifts toward people inside and outside the body of Christ. It is just a word to describe helping your friend build a retaining wall, fix his car, or till his yard. It means praying with a hurting associate, helping a person get a job, baby-sitting, or teaching a Bible study. A minister can share the facts of the Gospel or simply give a cup of cold water in the name of Christ. Ministry means extending the love of Christ to others, through the use of your supernatural tools.

A Commitment to Change

That Christians must accept a commitment to change goes almost without saying, but as soon as that goes unsaid, it goes undone.[3]

Paul states the unified purpose for each believer in both positive and negative terms. In Ephesians 4:13 he says the process of congregational maturation continues "until we . . . become mature, attaining to the whole measure of the fullness of Christ." Each believer has the objective of Christ-like-ness, to be striven for until he or she reaches heaven. Negatively, believers should ". . . no longer be infants, tossed back and forth by the waves, and blown here and there by every wind of teaching." They will also avoid ". . . the cunning and craftiness of men in their deceitful scheming" (v. 14).

At its core, the Christian life means Jesus Christ in every believer, living His life through us in the power of the Holy Spirit. Becoming more like Christ makes progress toward maturity mean something. When we are transferred to heaven, we will not become Christ or deity, but we will become Christ-like. With the sin removed from us, we will be perfect, glorified human beings.

To be an effective minister, I need the foundation of a Christ-like character and the preparation for the ministry. Preparation provides the skill, and Christ-like-ness provides the inner strength to use the skill.

Doctrinal Dualism. Many evangelicals practice a dangerous doctrinal dualism that springs out of the classic distinction between being and doing. Proponents of this theory teach that being is more important than doing and propose that being must go before doing. They teach that you need to build a deep relationship with Christ before you can effectively minister for Him. This dualism has a serious deleterious effect on Christians, because it slows their progress toward Christ-like-ness by setting up a false growth process.

Though they rightly warn against doing ministry without an inner commitment to Christ, these people have missed the fact that Christ taught that being and doing are interrelated and feed off each other. As one cynic put it, "Try being without doing." Christ gave His disciples small bits of information and then had them try it out. Then He would dispense more information and allow them to practice that.

The quickest and most effective means of teaching someone to swim is to give a few instructions on how to dog-paddle and throw him in the water. Likewise, character development does not occur in the monastic model. When people experience the challenge of the events of doing ministry, real learning takes place. Does a Christian learn more about teaching the Bible or answering philosophical questions by study in a sterile environment or by actual practice?

Don't fall into the trap of thinking, *I must study and meditate for a couple of years before I engage in service.* Study and meditation should take place in the context of the pressures and challenges of ministry. In fact one cannot become Christlike without becoming active in ministry from the beginning of Christian experience. Being that does not include doing does not exist.

A Commitment to the Discovery and Use of Gifts

Just as the body requires full use of its members to work at top capacity, the church requires every member to take part, unless it wants to be physically disabled.

Though a physically disabled person's courage in overcoming a handicap may inspire us, the needless disabling of the church evinces no such emotions. The church need not suffer any weakness in the body, and when it does it is entirely culpable. In many cases congregations have merely simulated life; if not for a few highly committed members and the person of Christ, they would have expired long ago.

The church operates at a low efficiency level because too few work. Everything the church needs resides in the undiscipled body members, but neglectful leaders have not provided the vision. Congregational members lack commitment to be prepared and grow in Christ. Some body members even remain ignorant of their gifts and cannot employ them. This violates the objective that makes a mighty discipling church: ". . . We will in all things grow up into him who is the Head, that is, Christ. From him the whole body, joined and held together by every supporting ligament, grows and builds itself up in love." When does this process take place? "As each part does its work" (4:15, 16).

When the church violates the Ephesians 4:12–16 priorities and practices, it suffers greatly. So much is not done by so many who could do it. Church leadership—overwhelmed by the sins of wastefulness, neglect, and taking the path of least resistance—becomes ineffective. Well over 50 percent of the average congregation is a ministry wasteland. People go unchallenged and untrained, unused and unfulfilled.

The Road to Maturity. Unlike the physical body, the spiritual body does not automatically come together and join as ligaments, tendons, bones, and muscles. Proactive choices of faith by congregational members make it happen. God has gifted believers for their part in ministry "as each part does its work" (Ephesians 4:16). Leadership holds the responsibility for teaching about spiritual gifts and providing testing and experiences to determine gifts. Congregation members must take action by learning and experimenting to find their gifts. The more active Christians are in doing these things, the more they try a variety of tasks, and the sooner they will know and develop their gifts.

Ephesians 4:12–16 explains the Christian road to maturity. In fact, it is the only promise of corporate maturity found in the Epistles. It is the heartbeat of the discipling church. For full employment to exist in the church, the body must have these priorities: leadership, preparation, character development, and gift discovery and use. When these are in place, the body experiences self-perpetuating growth and builds itself up in loving acts. Such a church naturally does what is healthy—it gets up and takes action. It loves the world by serving the needs around it, being sacrificial in work, principled in living, and magnetic in its personality. Daily it will add to its members those that are being saved.

A Commitment to the Spirit-Filled Walk

The fifth chapter of Ephesians begins with an exhortation for believers to imitate God. Unless He provides some supernatural resource, this seems a cruel expectation. Indeed, all the people's priorities and commitments would be useless fodder, if not for the Holy Spirit. Three elements make up the Spirit-filled walk.

To Be Filled. Only once in the New Testament, in Ephesians 5:18, does the Lord command us to "be filled with the Spirit." The Greek syntax makes it clear that this filling is an ongoing, moment-by-moment experience.[4] Being filled with the Holy Spirit requires an act of the will, based on faith. A disciple chooses to allow God to control his life at that moment. It is just that simple, just that mysterious.

How do you know you are filled, apart from the Word of God's assurance? Surely the Scriptures form the foundation of a Christian's confidence, but without evidence, we would have little comfort in the long run.

Display the Evidences. Four participles used in Ephesians 5:19–21 describe the inner attitudes of the Spirit-filled person:

> SPEAKING. Speaking has to do with how we relate to others. How we use the tongue in difficult situations is one of life's greatest exams on the Spirit's control.
> SINGING. Singing shows the attitude of worship. A Spirit-controlled believer worships God. His Spirit protects the Christian's tongue from gossip, slander, and other destructive behaviors and loosens it to praise and sing to the Lord. The Spirit-filled person has a song in his heart and a desire to speak in positive terms about God.
> GIVING THANKS IN EVERYTHING. Because of the way the Spirit-filled Christian looks at life, he can give thanks in all things. Viewing life through the lens of Scripture, he can see the good God is doing, even in the midst of negative happenings. I believe God cannot turn our bad into good until we thank Him.
> SUBMITTING. This means getting into the proper position in relation to those around us. Submission calls for us to serve the authorities in our lives as well as those over whom we have authority. In the Spirit of Christ we are called to serve others because He has served our needs.

The Spirit-filled disciple displays the inner qualities described in Ephesians 5:19–21. One with controlled and uplifting speech, positive praise of God, who sees the good in all of life, and shows submission and teachableness in relationships is indeed a miracle person.

To Pass the Tests. Not only do Christians in the discipling church display the above inner qualities, they show forth some very rigorous external ones as well. Six kinds of relationships represent the most telling tests: (1) wife to husband, (2) husband to wife, (3) child to parent, (4) parent to child, (5) employee to employer, (6) employer to employee. For each the only question on the test is a variation of "What am I like in the kinds of relationships that are most important to me?" It might be rephrased, "What am I like behind closed doors, as I relate to my mate?" "What am I like when I train my children?" "How do I treat employees?" "Do I give my employer a full day's work?" Above all, am I rebellious or submissive, mature or irresponsible, in these relationships?

The commitments Paul outlines in his letter to the Ephesians complement and expand the disciple's profile in John 15:7–17 and confirm the priorities and practices of the first church (Acts 2:42–47).

Clearly the teachings of Christ made two major transitions. First they made one from Christ to the first church. Then they went from first church, through Paul, to the discipling church at Ephesus. Though communicated in different terms and settings, the priorities and practices remained the same. Jesus' intentional strategy for discipling passed on to all His followers.

11
The Pastoral Priorities

The primary difference between the letters Paul wrote to the Ephesian church and Timothy is the responsibility of the recipient. The church populace needed to understand individual priorities; but leaders needed to think corporately and strategically, considering the larger management issues and developing the principles that guide the discipling process.

Though they lack homiletical style and mention a variety of subsidiary pastoral priorities, Paul's emotionally charged last words to his protégé yield three major leadership priorities in the discipling church:

Guarding the Gospel by commitment to the Word
Guarding the church by leadership development
Guarding the ministry by being a good model

GUARDING THE GOSPEL BY COMMITMENT TO THE WORD

"Guard the good deposit that was entrusted to you— guard it with the help of the Holy Spirit who lives in us" (2

Timothy 1:14). This, Paul's major charge to Timothy, entrusts him with guarding the sacred deposit, the Gospel.

All pastoral duties flow from this charge, and Scripture should drive pastoral work. Leaders must take action and engage in a series of practices that obey the Bible's teachings. Therefore Paul's exhortations concerning Timothy's relationship to the Word dominate this letter, and he outlines a threefold commitment to it.

Study God's Word

"Do your best to present yourself to God as one approved, a workman who does not need to be ashamed and who correctly handles the word of truth" (2 Timothy 2:15). The faithful pastor commits himself to studying and knowing the Word. As he stands before hearers, ready to present them with a gift of God's message, he should be a skilled craftsman.

Disappointingly, often the pastor does not give the Word a high priority in his work style. "Work style" does not mean preaching, but the manner in which a pastor conducts himself. What kinds of activities take up the lion's share of his time? Does he make training leaders a priority, spending time in ongoing meetings with them, or does he waste that time attending subsidiary board meetings, in order to keep both hands on the management wheel?

I believe the pastor whose schedule is driven by the Word of God will find the former option the best time stewardship. If we learn anything from the first-church experience, we see the commitment the apostles had to the ministry of the Word and prayer (Acts 6:1–7). If a pastor is driven by the Word, commitment to develop a church whose priorities and practices are driven by the Word should dominate his activity.

Too many pastors remain uncommitted to discipling because they have not committed themselves to the ministry of the Word. The leader who struggles with the Bible's teachings and determines what God wants done on that basis will emerge with a discipling view. If, however, he falls prey to a pragmatic lust to do what works, he has gone awhoring after other gods. For any church leader, ministry rightly begins with studying God's Word.

Some pastors commit themselves to studying the Word for sermon preparation and nothing else. I advocate serious study of God's Word for ministry strategy, goals, and ways to measure church activity. What does the Bible say about spiritual growth and how to measure it? Does it teach that every Christian is to witness, and if so, what can we do about it? What does it say about training Christians? The difference between the generic pastor and Paul's view of a pastor lies in the importance of studying for application, strategy, and the discipling process.

Teach God's Word

When necessary, Paul did not hesitate to lower the autocratic boom. Though he makes several charges to Timothy, he presents none more passionately than the responsibility to teach and preach. "Preach the Word; be prepared in season and out of season; correct, rebuke and encourage—with great patience and careful instruction" (2 Timothy 4:2).

"Preach" means more than delivering sermons to a Sunday-morning congregation. Though it includes such an event, the pastor's main function is communicating God's Word to others. Everything else grows out of this commitment.

Like "preaching," "be prepared" can and should apply to sermon preparation, but it also pertains to an attitude of spiritual readiness. "In season and out of season" implies "do it when it's convenient and when it's not."

Paul further exhorts Timothy to "correct, rebuke and encourage." These three words cover a wide range of Word-oriented activity. *Correct* does not imply the person is inherently unteachable. Correction can be done in gentleness, in a congenial environment. However, a leader employs *rebuke* when he addresses a problem of blatant, unconfessed sin. The major portion of Word activity involves *encourage,* since the majority of people need some gentle correction and a lot of encouragement.

All these Word-oriented activities are legitimate discipling, but how much does a church disciple? Since preaching is the first and most important step for local-church discipling, virtually all Bible-honoring pastors disciple to some extent. But are they trying to make disciples in a holistic, churchwide fashion?

Helping people by rebuking, correcting, and encouraging them is also discipling. But how extensively does a church engage in these? A built-in accountability program, esteemed churchwide, makes the teaching of the Word more effective. A lack of good application vehicles for Bible teaching makes much teaching yield less fruit than it should.

Paul ends his charge by mentioning "great patience and careful instruction." Young, timid, and impatient Timothy had complained, "These people make fun of my youth, and nobody listens to me." Paul told him, "Be patient with yourself and others. Indeed, take great pains with both your study and presentation of God's Word. It will pay big dividends."

The discipling-church pastor commits himself to the full-orbed ministry of the Word. The distinctive of such a pastor is that his teaching, applications, and total church strategy are derived from God's Word.

Let God's Word Direct the Entire Discipling Process

Second Timothy 3:16, 17, the discipling church's key text, provides Word-directed discipling process: "All Scripture is God-breathed and is useful for teaching, rebuking, correcting, and training in righteousness, so that the man of God may be thoroughly equipped for every good work." These verses describe the learning cycle for Christian development, which takes place in every growing believer; if it stalls out, growth becomes retarded. The discipling process finds its nexus in this text, which provides its source, process, and result.

The Source. True Christianity is Word driven. God chose to communicate to man in the form of symbols—words—that represent images in the mind. God inspired men to use these symbols to communicate His person and will. Using the vehicle of human personality and literary style, God supernaturally guided the biblical writers to write down these matters without error in the original form.

This teaching, known as inspiration, is derived in part from "all Scripture is God-breathed . . ." (3:16). True faith is Word driven because of the Word's Author. He has spoken to man through the written Word, which is to be our guide. Therefore we must begin, seek guidance for, and evaluate all ministry in the light of the Word.

Paul exhorted Timothy to study and teach the Word, and his exhortation remains for the modern pastor or leader. Anything less than leading and teaching the people of God based on the directions from God's Word is dereliction of duty.

The Results. When leaders engage in Word-driven ministry, they do so "so that the man of God may be thoroughly equipped for every good work" (3:17). The process is designed to prepare Christians for service. The discipling principles converge around one Greek word, *exertismenos,* translated "thoroughly equipped." This perfect passive participle communicates a completed action in the past, which has results that continue indefinitely into the future; the Word of God equips a person for a lifetime. The passive voice indicates that the equipped person is being acted on by the Word of God. By a faith choice the Christian receives the benefits of God; the participle indicates this is an ongoing process.

The Greek root of this word, *exartizo,* "fully equipped," is closely related to *katartizo,* translated "prepare" in Ephesians 4:12. Luke employs the same core word in Christ's statement ". . . everyone who is fully trained will be like his teacher" (Luke 6:40). "Fully trained" is the same root word.[1]

Around *exartizo* gather the teaching of Christ (Luke 6:40), the responsibility of the corporate church leadership (Ephesians 4:12), and the supernatural working of God's Word in the disciple's life (2 Timothy 3:16, 17). The issue is preparation for a life of service. Only the Word of God can prepare a person for effective ministry. Why would a Christian focus on any other means? Can't we call into question every ministry that is not Word directed, based on this truth alone?

The Word of God drives the discipling church, which prepares people to be healthy and productive. This naturally results in reproduction and multiplication. As the church keeps pushing the outer limits of mission, people are converted, the body grows, and God is glorified. I wish I knew why we find it so hard to live by these simple principles!

The Process. Paul prescribes a fourfold learning process: The Word of God is ". . . useful for teaching, rebuking, correcting and training in righteousness" (3:16). Each word represents a distinct part of the cycle.

1. Teaching. Didaskalian means "teaching or instruction." In this case it is used in a general sense to describe the principles God desires His people to follow. One might also express the same idea by saying that teaching the Word of God prescribes the path on which the disciple is to walk.

2. Rebuking. Our English word *rebuke* communicates more emotion than the Greek word *elenchon* warrants. We might more clearly describe its meaning as "conviction" in modern English, because the Greek word does not imply sternness or mean spiritedness. The Holy Spirit brings to light where we have departed from the prescribed path of teaching, and God's Spirit could not have either of those negatives. A preferable mental image of the word would be the Holy Spirit as helper, counselor, the paraclete, called alongside to help. God puts his arm around us, points out our error, and tells us where to proceed from there.

Chart 7
The Fourfold Learning Cycle

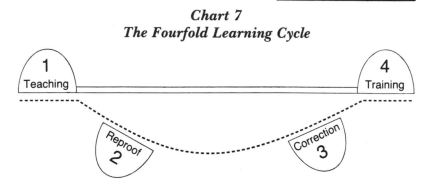

Sadly, many Christians get the first step, teaching, and they sin. They repeat the cycle, getting more teaching and sinning some more. But they never move on to the long-term correction of their problem, though God has pointed the way out to them.

3. Correcting. Epanorthosin means "to set up straight on your feet." This Greek word presents us with part of a vivid picture: a person walking on a prescribed path (teaching) leaves the path and stumbles down into a culvert (rebuking). Now he must stand up and get back on the prescribed path (correction).

The Scriptures tell us what to do, rebuke us when we don't do it, and admonish us to get back on the path. This corrective process shows the importance of accountability, for you cannot hold people accountable without God's revelation. The spiritual leader who cannot invoke the authority of God's Word has no portfolio, no place in which he can plant his feet, take a stand, and hold off the opposition. Corrective ministry is vital to successful discipling.

Damaged goods. Sin destroys; it eats away at a person's self-worth, erodes confidence, and leaves emotional and physical scars. Often, after having a serious bout with evil, a person needs help getting back on track. Like a traveler who has fallen asleep at the wheel and crashed into a ditch, a Christian may not be able to extricate himself from the wreckage. Others need to rescue him, carry him to the road, place him in an ambulance, and take him to a hospital. Once the doctors have cared for him through surgery and medicine, the physical therapists may provide exercises that will return normal locomotion.

Scripture not only tells us we have departed from God's path, it helps put us back together again. Correction could mean reading Philippians 4 and learning how to deal with anxiety. Or God might challenge the Christian to overcome depression, using the formula God gave Elijah in 1 Kings 17. Whatever problem a Christian faces, Scripture can provide clear corrective measures.

4. Training. Paideian means "instruction with discipline." Most often modern educators associate the word *training* with young people, but in a way *paideia* captures the entire process of Christian development. It joins information with discipline or accountability; this gradual, ongoing process is intentional and guided. In Chapter 2, I defined discipling as "The intentional training of Christians, with accountability, on the basis of loving relationships." If someone required me to write that definition in New Testament Greek, I would use *paideia* for "training."

The way I understand it, training is teaching, and teaching is training. Though I have used *training* as a generalized word, merely meaning "to set forth the right information," it also includes the idea of teaching a student through repeated experience, while keeping a watchful eye on him. Jesus' six-step teaching method best exemplifies training in righteousness.

While Paul's admonition concerning demonstration, imitation, and reproduction (1 Thessalonians 1:5–8) gives us the discipling process from the fellowship lounge, 2 Timothy

3:16, 17 provides the view from the engine room. For ministry to work effectively, both must take place, but a valid ministry is Word driven. If the fuel of ministry is not channeled through the engine room, the ship lies dead in the water. Passengers in the fellowship lounge can keep on having a wonderful time—but only until they run out of food and water. When the ship stops making progress because of problems in the engine room, eventually the vision dies, the passengers bicker among themselves, and the cause is lost.

Far too many churches frolic about the lounge, not yet having noticed that the ship has come to a standstill. They may be trapped in a never-ending cycle of teaching and rebuke, but because they have resisted accountability, no one can employ corrective ministry. *Paideia* requires accountability. Training people means rolling up your sleeves, getting involved; leaders must know where they are going and have the courage to measure their goals by biblical standards.

Paul's fourfold learning cycle is just that—a cycle. It takes place myriads of times in thousands of areas in our lives. Only by engaging God and His Word in all four phases can we fully develop. Only when a church does so corporately can it reach maturity in Christ and ministry.

GUARDING THE CHURCH BY LEADERSHIP DEVELOPMENT

Church leaders need to have two things: foundational spiritual qualities and leadership skills. Foundational spiritual qualities are character, faithfulness, and spiritual gifts. Multiplying leaders also have six ministry skills: They can effectively communicate Scripture, can articulate the philosophy of disciple making, can manage or coach others, can motivate others, can correct others, and are effective in evangelism.[2]

The above principles are rooted in Scripture, but how a

leader presents them is a matter of personal taste and style. Paul provides Timothy with leadership qualifications and personal opinions about their application. Here are the simplest, broadest principles he gave the discipling church at Ephesus (1 Timothy 3:1–16; 5:17–21).

Leadership Must Be Proven Faithful

Paul expressed concern that Timothy would guard the sacred deposit of the Gospel. He was to be careful whom he trusted with it: "And the things you have heard me say in the presence of many witnesses entrust to reliable men who will also be qualified to teach others" (2 Timothy 2:2).[3]

Leadership is to be entrusted with the Gospel, not subsidiary church work. Yet how many congregational power brokers have no direct relationship to the teaching or passing on of the Gospel? In our materialistic society, power is money, and people who have money or control money are often considered spiritual leaders. This concept is foreign to Paul's thinking.

To cure such a malady, require all potential leaders to submit to a course of study and accountability applications directly related to learning the Gospel and reproducing themselves through it. The communication and reproduction of the Gospel must become the criteria for leadership. A candidate must be spiritually motivated and propagating the Gospel must become his ultimate objective. Start an apprentice with simple and undemanding tasks, and slowly move him on to more complex objectives. Any leader must prove his faithfulness through his actions (Luke 16:10). This easy rule is often violated: If the would-be leader doesn't complete the simple things, don't move him on to difficult tasks. Ignoring this maxim has destroyed many a leader, an unfaithful follower, and a ministry.

Reliability is a nonnegotiable for leadership. Many pastors and leaders complain about unfaithful fellow leaders. The unfaithful come to meetings late or simply don't come at all. They don't fulfill their responsibilities, lack motivation, and after a full term on the board, never want to serve again. Such an entire leadership picture, on a wide scale, spells frustration.

This leadership scenario plays out simply because the church has not taken Paul's advice to Timothy seriously. People don't seem to want to take the time and energy to make faithfulness a priority. I believe they don't know how to implement a plan and make it happen.

Because of the relational problems it creates, changing what is and culling out the unfaithful can prove a difficult task. But pastors have no choice but to address the issue if they want to obey God. Leaders who want faithful men through whom they can reproduce and pass on the Gospel must start by being faithful themselves. The elementary grades for leadership development are demonstrated in faithfulness. Passing over such foundational issues compares to sending a five-year-old to high school. Do that, and you pay the price.

Leadership Must Be Character Qualified

First Timothy 3:1–16 is second nature to the principles of this book because it represents nineteen practical life-application qualifications for leaders. A few ministry skills, such as "able to teach," appear, because this repeats the qualifications for faithful men (2 Timothy 2:2). Several times the list mentions management skills. For example, a leader should manage his household, family, and business affairs well. That does not call for the gift of administration, but it does mean a leader watches over his main responsibilities.

What weight should we assign these qualifications? Almost anyone will admit such qualifications exist and consider them important, but today's church has a common propensity for placing them in the same category as the Lord's Prayer, 1 Corinthians 13, the Beatitudes, and the Ten Commandments: "They are wonderful guides, but if we held people to that, no one would lead."

True, no one measures up 100 percent, but we should not allow perfectionism to hold qualifications hostage. Neither should we allow fatalistic cynicism to dampen our enthusiasm for pursuing them.

Some will dismiss the application of these qualifications under the guise of the impossibility of their attainment, employing the "nobody's perfect" excuse or the cynical "you've got to be kidding" technique. To take qualifications seriously entails overcoming the resistance to their application. Excuses usually cover fear and ignorance.

Taking this passage seriously means developing a training program for potential leaders and coaching all willing trainees toward effective application of the character qualities extolled in the text. Train them, coach them, measure them, screen them; then you are being serious.

The Old Testament describes the custom of the elders sitting at the city gates, where they engage in dialogue with sages. For the church, I would like to expand that image to the elders, guarding the gates of the church. Intentional leadership development, based on taking scriptural qualifications seriously, protects the church from evil.

Leadership development gives the church philosophical purity at the leadership level. Philosophical purity means top leadership essentially agrees on doctrine, ministry philosophy, and methodology. Such unity makes it more difficult for the enemy to drive a wedge between leaders.

Leaders do better work and ministry when they have thoroughly proven themselves and had thorough schooling before assuming a post. Leadership development provides the church with outstanding examples of the church's goals. The most powerful teaching tool combines knowledge and example of knowledge application; if church leaders live out the teachings and priorities of the church, others will follow.

Good doctrine and Scripture are not enough; they must be joined by a commitment to leadership development. A pastor who does not reproduce himself by building leaders is an unfaithful shepherd: He has abandoned his post to pursue other gods.

Leaders Must Be Accountable

You can't make disciples without accountability, and the need for accountability never ends. While elders need less watching than most people, they must be responsible for their actions. What happens when an elder falls, and the church and the watching world hear and see it? It brings shame to Christ, His people, and their cause. The fallen is also sidelined from the leadership position. Elder accountability remains so crucial because the price tag for failure is so high.

First Timothy 5:17, 18 tells Timothy to make sure elders who are doing well receive honor, and those who labor at preaching and teaching should receive double honor. However, with honor comes the flip side, the cost of leadership. If you expect honor, expect higher standards.

In dealing with accusations against elders, Paul continues, warning, "Do not entertain an accusation against an elder unless it is brought by two or three witnesses" (5:19). One of the awful things about spiritual leadership is the stories people make up about you. Most readers will have experienced innovative fabrications concerning themselves and their families. Satan can always find people in the church willing to slander leaders, tell half-truths, and throw in a bit of innuendo. Paul warns Timothy to simply ignore much of the "storied garbage" slung around by church people. If there is truth to what is said, there are witnesses to it who are willing to come forward: "Those who sin are to be rebuked publicly, so that the others may take warning" (5:20).

When an elder sins seriously and brings shame to Christ and His church, immediate action should be taken. He should receive a rebuke in front of everyone, because his position means he casts a shadow of sin over the entire congregation. In many instances, leaders have lost their courage and have not gone public; they want to sweep the sin under the rug, because it might make the church look bad. In reality, when they do this, the offender becomes a martyr. The only way a man can be restored is by confessing his sin, naming it to the entire group he has offended, and receiving their forgiveness.

If an elder confesses his sin and repents, he should name the sin to the entire congregation and not be rebuked. Other elders should recommend restoration to fellowship, but not to leadership.

Elders Hold Other Elders Accountable. Part of the accountability side of leadership development takes place at the elder level. Many areas of elders' lives need fine-tuning, but often these issues do not surface until one experiences power with responsibility. Authority to make decisions carries a responsibility that causes our strengths to become weaknesses. For example, a person who pays close attention to detail has an important role in a working team of spiritual leaders, but when that ability to focus on detail becomes nit-picking, it impedes progress by frustrating others and creating tension. Elders need to become accountable to one another in character-development issues as well as in fulfilling responsibilities and completing tasks.

The Final Charge. "I charge you, in the sight of God and Christ Jesus and the elect angels, to keep these instructions without partiality, and to do nothing out of favoritism" (1 Timothy 5:21). When Paul wants to make an unusually deep impression, he takes a running start by picturing the entire heavenly host as on-site observers. To do nothing from favoritism and maintain impartiality are two ways of saying, "Be objective!" "These instructions" probably refers to both the treatment of elders and the entire set of preceding instructions. Like Paul's charges to flee lust and pursue a pure life (1 Timothy 6:11–14) and to preach the Gospel (2 Timothy 4:1–3), this command carries some weight.

How many churches openly sin by not intentionally developing leaders? How many objectively select leaders? Paul solemnly tells us to develop leaders, because it guards the church and makes ministry more effective. Without a clear objective, a training program, and an impartial screening program that measures objective character and skill qualities, the church has not taken seriously the charge to develop leaders. All that is left is the "good ol' boy" system, filled with favoritism and partiality. Real leadership development requires that we follow Paul's instructions.

GUARDING THE MINISTRY BY BEING A GOOD MODEL

"People are watching." "Everything we do teaches." "Vision is more caught than taught." Many axiomatic expressions emphasize the importance of modeling. Likewise Scripture teaches the importance of a good example. Peter called leaders to be good examples to the flock (1 Peter 5:3). Paul encouraged others, including Timothy, to imitate him as he did Christ (Philippians 4:9; 1 Corinthians 11:1). Timothy did just that.

Separated from them by hundreds of miles, from Ephesus, Paul writes to the Corinthians, "Therefore I urge you to imitate me." Are the Corinthians to do this based on memory? No, Paul will send Timothy. "For this reason"—because they need to imitate, but Paul could not come himself—"I am sending to you Timothy, my son whom I love, who is faithful in the Lord. He will remind you of my way of life in Christ Jesus . . ." (1 Corinthians 4:16, 17). Timothy had imitated Paul; now the Corinthians could imitate the apostle by watching Timothy. In fact, by imitating Paul, they imitated Christ.

Paul did not encourage them to imitate his personality; he wanted the Corinthians to imitate a body of truth and a philosophy of ministry. At the end of verse 17, Paul describes the model he passed on to the Corinthians: ". . . which agrees with what I teach everywhere in every church." I believe he refers to the same body of teaching he described in 2 Timothy: "What you heard from me, keep as the pattern of sound teaching, with faith and love in Christ Jesus. Guard the good deposit that was entrusted to you—guard it with the help of the Holy Spirit who lives in us" (1:13, 14).

Paul had a standardized truth he taught in every church he visited. The core data would have been the message of Christ as Messiah; the subsidiary teaching would have been the Great Commission and its applications. His teachings on spiritual gifts, the body ministry, qualifications for leaders, and so on was all Gospel, and we can read the how-to manual by piecing together his writings.

The Corinthians were to imitate Timothy's doctrine and his application to personal life and the church. They were to learn by observing him. Paul gave Timothy clear details about what those things should include:

> Set an example for the believers in speech, in life, in love, in faith and in purity.
>
> 1 Timothy 4:12

> . . . Flee from all this, and pursue righteousness, godliness, faith, love, endurance and gentleness. Fight the good fight of the faith. Take hold of the external life to which you were called when you made your good confession in the presence of many witnesses.
>
> 1 Timothy 6:11, 12

> You, however, know all about my teaching, my way of life, my purpose, faith, patience, love, endurance, persecutions, sufferings. . . . But as for you, continue in what you have learned and have become convinced of, because you know those from whom you learned it.
>
> 2 Timothy 3:10, 11, 14

Model Convictions. I have often said, "Laugh at my ideas, scoff at my opinions, but don't mess with my convictions." Convictions are the beliefs I'm willing to fight for. Leaders should model what they have learned and have convictions about. Bone-deep beliefs concerning ethics and philosophy become infectious, and others follow personal convictions concerning ministry.

Setting a good example will protect the integrity of your ministry. Personal life-style and ethics form the foundation of any work for God. Others will model themselves after your example, so make sure what you reproduce is desirable.

12
Development of a Leadership Community

Every discipling church will eventually develop a leadership community; indeed, it *must* in order to move into reproduction and multiplication. The church that wants to move into "Come and be with Me" needs one.

Leaders and their apprentices comprise the local church's leadership community, which seeks to accomplish four things:

1. Develop instruction/teaching
2. Create application vehicles
3. Strategize for outreach/church planting
4. Provide an apprenticeship environment

Though some people might call this a training center, a seminary, or even a church-planting school, these terms miss the real essence of the word *community*. The leadership community is a group of spiritually and relationally fused people, working together in the cause for Christ.

The leadership community is not for everyone. To enter the "Come and be with Me" phase of leadership training, a person must receive an invitation to participate and make a commitment to the community's rules and requirements. A small portion of the Ephesian congregation became part of Paul's leadership community. (Normatively 10 percent of a church's worship attendance becomes part of the leadership community.) How and why did he begin a leadership community?

FROM INSTITUTIONALISM TO INSTITUTING

After three months of dialogue in the local synagogue, Paul exchanged stained glass for a chalkboard. Many synagogue leaders had become obstinate, maligning Paul and his teachings. So the apostle practiced a principle many of us should heed: Work with the seekers, the spiritually well; don't allow the disobedient to dictate ministry strategy. Paul transformed his outreach into a classroom, forming his own leadership institute in the lecture hall of Tyrannus. For two years, from 11:00 A.M. to 4:00 P.M., Paul held daily discussions: "Paul worked at tent making during the cool of the morning and public life stopped at 11:00 A.M. and with it Tyrannus's lectures. Paul took over the school and took on all comers."[1]

Understand Paul's clientele: ". . . He took the disciples with him" (Acts 19:9). The general Ephesian congregation did not follow, just a special group of apprentices, candidates for leadership of future ministries and churches. They formed a leadership community that would lead to the evangelization of the entire region of Asia: ". . . So that all the Jews and Greeks who lived in the province of Asia heard the word of the Lord" (Acts 19:10).

A leadership community seeks to expand the boundaries and reach of Christianity. Members are driven by the Great

Chart 8
The Discipling Church

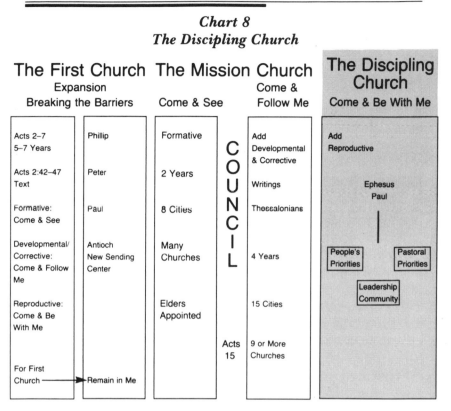

The First Church Expansion Breaking the Barriers		The Mission Church Come & See	Come & Follow Me		The Discipling Church Come & Be With Me
Acts 2–7 5–7 Years	Phillip	Formative	**C**	Add Developmental & Corrective	Add Reproductive
Acts 2:42–47 Text	Peter	2 Years	**O**	Writings	Ephesus Paul
Formative: Come & See	Paul	8 Cities	**U** **N** **C**	Thessalonians	
Developmental/ Corrective: Come & Follow Me	Antioch New Sending Center	Many Churches	**I** **L**	4 Years	People's Priorities Pastoral Priorities
Reproductive: Come & Be With Me		Elders Appointed		15 Cities	Leadership Community
For First Church ──►	Remain in Me		Acts 15	9 or More Churches	

Commission and held together by a commitment to Christ and His cause.

Leadership-Community Goals

1. Develop Instruction/Teaching. Jesus had chosen the twelve for two reasons: ". . . That they might be with him," that is, so that the modeling and character transference foundational to the discipling process might occur; and "that he might send them out to preach," that is, so that they might develop ministry skills (Mark 3:14). Taking his lead from Jesus, Paul plans to influence his select disciples by his person and philosophy. He takes those who have traveled with him or have excelled since his coming to Ephesus and places them in a special environment that will produce leaders.

Some refer to Paul's instruction as teaching/evangelism. The word in Acts 19:9 translated "discussions," *dialegomenos,* means "to dispute or argue." "In rabbinic Judaism and in early Christianity there was no such clear-cut distinction between the work of the evangelist and the teacher."[2] A variety of scholars drew the inference that teaching evangelism was very common among the early church fathers such as Tatian and Clement. "These men were no dons, writing their Apologies in safety and at leisure. They were missionaries, preachers, evangelists, and in many cases, martyrs."[3] Paul's example in the lecture hall of Tyrannus provided the inspiration for the church fathers' approach.

Intellectual liveliness characterized Paul's teaching. He presented ideas from Scripture, peppered with polemics from himself and many students and seekers. *Dialegomenos* is used of the persuading power of his addresses. Daily he experienced encounters with the hostile and the hungry, both of whom could ask very difficult questions. The actual dialogue, debate, passion, and give-and-take provided the disciples with a very challenging learning environment.

Paul's objective was to do evangelism while he trained apprentices. Anyone who is going to reproduce a product or method must understand the philosophy that undergirds it. So Paul ran a street seminary of sorts; he trained "people scholars," men much like himself, who could shoot from the hip. Paul could dialogue with those who opposed him because he had been well taught. Likewise, his students learned principles and immediately put them to use. Nothing works more effectively than others' challenge to get a student to dig into the Word for answer.

Teach a philosophy that will last a lifetime. First I intentionally place a biblically based philosophy that will last a lifetime into a future leader. Methods may come and go, but underlying the principles that drive the method give a person emotional and ministry endurance. Paul spoke of the pattern of sound teaching he taught in every church. He wanted to reproduce that pattern of thinking in every church he planted, every pastor he commissioned, and every believer baptized.

Whatever method you use to teach the Gospel, crystallize your teachings into transferable and reproducible pieces. In our day of general biblical illiteracy, future leaders need a thorough grounding in the basic doctrines of Scripture. Present-day cultural conditions do not allow for debate and evangelism in the leadership community, but the instruction can and must take place there, beginning the transformation of a person by the renewing of his mind. Principles sustain a person during a lifetime of ministry.

2. Create Application Vehicles. True teaching always creates application vehicles. The leadership community is the place for step five of Christ's six-step method, "Let them do it."

Paul's lecture hall provided a forum for instruction in philosophical foundations and application. The hall contained three groups of people: the disciples, or apprentices; the seekers, those who would eventually come to faith; and the opponents, who tried to destroy the way. This mix provided an apologist's delight. Paul could start with a presentation. Opponents would challenge interpretations; the seekers would ask penetrating questions. Then Paul would answer and debate through the Scriptures. Disciples could immediately apply what they learned.

At first Paul answered most of the questions; possibly Timothy, Luke, Silas, or one of the leaders made a contribution. In time I suppose others took on some of the questions. It would also make perfect sense that they broke into smaller discussion groups, around various topics, giving apprentices the opportunity to articulate their views and hone their communicative skills. Because of the circumstances, Paul could "let them do it" while he observed.

Contemporary culture does not provide the kind of environment the hall of Tyrannus had. Opponents do not stroll into church buildings and dialogue with a speaker. Working people cannot take five hours from the middle of their day to learn in the manner of the Ephesians. But the same work needs to be done and the same principles need to be applied.

Unless they have a place to practice, people don't learn well. In my church we start apprentices as small-group assistants; there they learn the philosophical essentials and are given hands-on jobs. We want them to experience testing, to face the "friendly fire" of the members of their groups. We also expect them to share their faith and reach out to the people with whom they live, work, and play. The goal is for them to lead a group and train their own apprentices to lead groups. In this system, everyone reproduces every year; that keeps the leadership community alive and growing.

Paul could not have lectured five hours a day, six days a week, for two years, anyway. How do I know that? Two reasons come to mind, one practical, the other scripturally founded. If five-hour lectures in the heat of the day held people's interest, I would question if their IQs exceeded room temperature. They had to do more than listen to theological presentations.

To the debate and discussion I believe went on in the hall, skeptics probably responded, "So what?" The Bible's "so that" answers their question: ". . . So that all the Jews and Greeks who lived in the province of Asia heard the word of the Lord" (Acts 19:10). Clearly Luke considered the meetings in the hall of Tyrannus the reason the message of Christ reached the entire province. What took place in Paul's leadership community made reaching people and church planting possible. That required more outreach than simple lecturing would have provided.

Field trips, anyone? When Paul was not lecturing, he went to the streets, ministering: "God did extraordinary miracles through Paul" (19:11). "Many of those who believed now came and openly confessed their evil deeds. . . . The word of the Lord spread widely and grew in power" (19:18, 20). I think Paul took his disciples and hit the streets for ministry, because in his charge to the Ephesian elders at Miletus, he speaks of ministering for three years ". . . from house to house" (20:20).

For a time the mix of seekers, disciples, and opponents in the lecture hall provided the disciples with a mental stretch, but after a while the seekers had their questions answered, the skeptics had their objections soundly rejected, and the disciples could answer questions and reject arguments. Paul knew it was time for the next step, and they took the truth they had learned to the world.

3. Strategize for Outreach/Church Planting. How can we apply the leadership community to the contemporary church culture? There are three ways to develop outreach and church planting:

> Network church events
> Deploy the leadership community into local outreach
> Church planting

Network church events. The single greatest need and advantage of the leadership community is that it provides the pastor with a regular opportunity to keep the vision before his ministry core. Loss of the people's vision and zeal for what God can do among them sinks so many churches. So daily Paul infused his followers with the promises, commands, and challenges that needed to be regularly before the church.

In many churches, hundreds of events just happen, without much input: Bible studies, retreats, picnics, hoedowns, recreational leagues, special groups for special needs, and so on. What if the leadership community really got behind each event and used it as an outreach to the unchurched? Say the leadership community consists of the leaders and their apprentices, people from 25 groups, representing a congregation of 250. Youth leaders, junior high workers, and other segments of the community will have representatives, too.

Suppose that leadership community joins together and tries to reach into their networks of members and get every person they can to a retreat. As a result, 100 more women attend the retreat than ever before. If the leadership community plans ahead to have four women close the retreat with an offer to continue the retreat's spiritual high by forming four small groups, beginning the next week, new networks will have been formed. Use the natural networks of your church to gather increased numbers of people. (For more information on forming small-group networks—the primary way the leadership community lives and functions—read the Appendix, which will explain this system in detail.)

Deploy the leadership community into local outreach. Paul took his men to the streets; in our day, the path to the streets leads through the natural networks of small-group membership.

Our small groups start with high support, addressing many felt needs. Though I do not support allowing felt need to drive ministry, I am willing to enter people's lives through the felt-need door. Recently I heard of a church that was started from a seminar offered on potty training. Granted, parents of toddlers have this major need, but it is a short-lived window of opportunity. The fact that so many attend shows how short-lived everyone wants it to be!

When they are productive and done in good taste, I favor and support evangelistic events that gather people to hear a direct Gospel presentation. The far better way, however, is to train people to walk down the paths of their lives, where, quite naturally, they find people who need Christ. Training people in small groups to do event evangelism did not work across the board for us. People could not translate the event skills into the natural flow of their lives. When they left the groups, they stopped planning events, because they just didn't find it practical.

Changing our style, we helped Christians network more effectively and began to give them credit for watering the neighbors' lawn, when they went on a vacation. We said it counted as outreach when someone took a friend to a baseball game, helped him landscape his yard, or baby-sat his children. This laid the foundation for future talks and opportunities to lead that friend to Christ.

However, our main charge was to open the small groups. Previous groups had been closed for reasons of training, meeting special needs, and so on. Most of our people faced the obstacle of where to gather with the unchurched—they lacked a natural vehicle into which they could take people. The most natural place was the small group.

To the seeker, unchurched, and the Christian looking for a church home, the Christian can naturally say, "Would you like to come to my small group?" Ninety percent of all people attend a church because a friend brought them. If the church only provides closed groups, where can members bring friends? Time probably does not allow the Christian to add another group to his schedule, and his friend will not go alone, so in a closed-group system, nothing happens.

Our leadership community believes gathering people is a team effort and tries to assimilate others into the community, the church environment. Joe is interested in knowing more about Christ, and he loves golf. I am Joe's friend, but

I hate golf. Because I know three men in my church network who love golf and Christ and would love Joe, I introduce them, and Joe becomes bonded to them; he therefore finds Christ within our church community.

Without a leadership community to feed these values and methods, none of this evangelism will occur. Local outreach depends upon the leadership community's energy, guidance, and accountability. The pastor and a team of coordinators direct the leadership community. In Paul's team, Timothy, Silas, and Luke were coordinators; they would have had a team of apprentices under their direction. Each apprentice, in turn, had a group of several people and apprentices. The leadership community's arms reach deep into the congregation, and it has the ability to reach hundreds of lives. With its regular meetings, it can monitor, make adjustments, remove problem people, move in new leaders, and provide ongoing direction essential to outreach success. The leadership community's energy and passion give the church's bloodstream a passionate vitality.

Church planting. When a local church becomes a discipling church, it does not stop outreach at the city limits. Under Paul's direction, the Ephesian leadership community expanded into the whole province of Asia. The six sister churches that join Ephesus and undergo Christ's scrutiny in Revelation 2, 3 are the fruit of the Ephesian church's leadership community.

Paul did not consider evangelism without church planting; it would never have occurred to him that one could exist without the other. When Christ is preached in a region, and you plan to stay and follow through, the natural and necessary conclusion is a local church.

Most people believe that the most effective means to reach people for Christ lies in church planting, but I don't think Paul said, "Let us go plant churches." I think he said, "Go, preach Christ, and if the work bears fruit, form a church."

Some present-day church planting has misguided notions about starting a new church. Often a person says, "I am going to plant a church in Joytown. I will find a place where there are not too many good churches, find interested Christians, and begin." Such a leader mainly focuses on forming a church, not drawing people to Christ. I think his language indicates starting churches means more to him than preaching Christ does. If he sets a goal of starting a church, once he has enough Christians in the church to support him, he may feel satisfied. Paul would have preached Christ to those who needed him and would have shaped a new church around new Christians. If a leader does not plant churches to reach the unconverted, why is he doing it?

Challenge your best and brightest apprentices to leave home areas for the missions and church planting. A discipling church should discuss, plan for, and partly finance church planting.

4. Provide an Apprenticeship Environment. A careful accounting of on-site personnel yields the fact that twenty-seven people, from Pontus, Rome, Alexandria, Macedonia, Thessalonica, Iconium, Corinth, Laodicea, and Colossae, are named as leadership-community members during Paul's stay in Ephesus. This does not even take into account the previously confirmed members: Luke, Silas, Timothy, and Erastus. Excluding the general-populace disciples of Ephesus, the group numbered over thirty.

Every area where Paul had preached and established a church had a representative in the leadership community. This kept the vision burning in the various churches and further developed the men in residence. For Paul, it provided accountability in each church he had founded. Most important, this method provided a reproducible model they could develop in their own churches and we can use in ours.

The leadership community sets the table for reproduction. A congregation becomes a mature discipling church when it reaches the "Come and be with Me" stage on a corporate level. On a small, unintentional scale, every church has some of this, but the discipling church knowingly and corporately develops this priority.

STARTING AND RUNNING A LEADERSHIP COMMUNITY

The Objective

As a church leader, you must set the goal of forming a ministry-leadership core from which you can create, direct, and expand the church's ministry through evangelism, church planting, and world mission. You will also train leaders who reproduce, multiply, and provide the church with a great team of leaders. The by-products in the church include passion, direction, quality control, and fruitfulness in its outreach to its own Jerusalem.

Choosing Personnel

Begin with your Silas, Timothy, and Luke types: those who have already proven themselves faithful and effective. These will become the core of the leadership community and will take on the various departments that develop. Generally such men are already on the elder-training track. They have made the commitments and have the desire for leadership mentioned in 1 Timothy 3:1.

If you cannot identify such a group in your church, move on to developing apprentices. An apprentice is willing to submit to the leadership-community training process. He must have demonstrated a variety of attributes and aptitudes. You might ask these questions about any would-be apprentice:

1. Does he desire to be part of the leadership community?
2. Does his heart burn for the same thing mine does?
3. Are his gifts appropriate for leadership?
4. Has he been tested in faithfulness and small tasks?
5. Is he teachable?

6. What would happen to his spiritual life if he became a leadership-community dropout? Is he emotionally stable?
7. Is he presently needed in the leadership community?

Once you have discussed these questions, if current members of your leadership community agree a person is qualified, you may invite him to the leadership community. Ask the apprentice to agree to sign a simple agreement. Requiring a commitment and time involvement should eliminate those who want to be part of the fun but do not want the work. Paul had weeded out the uncommitted by lecturing during the heat of the day. In order for people to give up the usual rest period at 1:00 P.M., they had to have commitment. You may weed out the modern-day equivalent of the sleepers by asking for the following commitments from each:

1. I desire to be part of the leadership community.
2. I desire to be trained in character and skills for future leadership.
3. I am willing to submit myself to the projects and environmental culture of the leadership community.
4. I will come on time to every meeting.
5. I am willing to commit myself to stay in the leadership community as long as I have ministry responsibility.

Some apprentices will sign the agreement, only to challenge it later. So many unexpected things can happen that, if it seems at odds with the apprentice's perception of what he signed, he will resist: "I didn't expect this. I don't read this into the contract." Use this opportunity to teach the apprentice an important truth of life: If he is only willing to fulfill commitments that are completely written out in detail, he is hedging on his commitments.

By the same reasoning marriage partners could opt out of their commitment because jobs such as taking out the trash and cleaning up after the kids weren't in the vows. "I didn't know you would get sick; I didn't know you were this messy. This wasn't in the contract." People who truly love have a commitment to each other. If an apprentice's heart burns for Christ, his spirit of commitment continues, even in the face of the difficult and unexpected. Don't start a leadership community thinking such battles are a possibility—they are a certainty.

Choosing personnel becomes critical for the leadership community. Remember, don't invite someone into the community unless you need him and have some responsibility for him. Don't invite him unless a current member believes strongly he should be there and that member will take the responsibility for apprenticing him. Don't invite anyone into the leadership community unless the pastor or director agrees.

A leadership community should start small and bring in new apprentices as the ministry grows. Ours started with a handful, grew to twelve, then fifteen, and soon will be over twenty. In the next two years, we expect it will number fifty or more.

How Does It Work?

The Format. The leadership community meets twice a month, at the time suited to your schedule. For the last two years, we have used Monday evening, from 5:30 to 7:30 P.M. A biweekly schedule provides regularity, but allows core leaders to work with their people during alternate weeks. Taking a month off in the summer is also a good idea.

The Agenda. This will change as the group grows, but you should follow some basic principles.

First hour. Begin with a fifteen-minute transitional period that allows people to wind down from a day's work. Refreshments or our favorite, a pizza supper, is recommended. For the next forty-five minutes, the pastor or director should give some kind of instruction. Teaching is vital; it can take the form of storytelling, vision casting, a theological presentation, or dialogue and debate concerning a relevant issue. The time could also be given to passing out awards for outstanding performance, praying for group members' needs, communion, or other forms of worship. During this, the director's time, the entire group stays together. He may also chose to brainstorm and network outreach ministries.

Second hour. At this time your Tituses, Timothys, and Silases take the people they work with and break into huddle groups to monitor specific ministries. Small-group leaders are taught group dynamics, and apprentices receive more basic instruction. As many as seven or eight huddle groups may meet simultaneously. For more details on how to use the second hour, see the Appendix.

Regardless of where you are in ministry, you can develop a leadership community. If you want to follow the traditions of Jesus, the first church, the mission church, and the discipling church, you will need a leadership community. Begin by getting your key people together and challenging them to become a leadership community, as outlined in this chapter.

While you develop a leadership community, it will continually change. The principles remain the same, but you will alter methods to fit the expertise and needs in your group and church. Start slowly and master the basic techniques before you experiment. Thoroughly school church leaders in discipling practices, so they can adapt other methods to what they already know.[4]

Commit yourself to reproducing and multiplying through the leadership community; train your leaders. Over the years, the cream will rise to the top, and God will give you many church planters, pastors, and missionaries.

By using this vehicle to teach leaders, you will unify them in purpose, philosophy, and strategy. Though personality and sin problems creep into the best teams, you will not have major wedges concerning purpose and function driven between leaders.

Once you have created a discipling church, you must manage a deployed church. When Paul spent four years in prison, his leadership continued to evangelize. From a distance he carried on through the people he had trained, and the churches did not suffer the way many modern congregations do when the pastor leaves and no one can effectively carry on the work. When a discipler sets the process into motion, there are enough personnel to carry on the work. Paul sat in prison, but as he aptly put it, ". . . But God's word is not chained" (2 Timothy 2:9). Trained men and women unleashed it on the world.

Paul's letters provided corrective action for the church, and in his apostles he dealt with the recipients' most important needs. These letters are rich with theology and practical advice. They touch on just about every issue that concerned the church then and now. They carry his message to a deployed church.

Part V

THE PRINCIPLES OF A GROWING CHURCH

The church did not develop by accident or from a purely miraculous collection of circumstances, apart from human action. God had a plan for the growth of the church, which Jesus exemplified in His ministry, but people had to carry on the work. As the apostles followed God's plan, working it out in each church they founded, the Word spread, and people came to Christ. Such expansion never took place as a result of disobedience, carelessness, or only by mistake.

In the growth of the young church, we can see how eight principles Jesus had shown his disciples fueled the church's expansion. These worked in the first century, and they can work today, too. As we add them to the priorities and practices we have already studied, we develop a framework around which we can form a discipling church.

13
The Well-Principled Church

As well as exemplifying the four discipleship stages, Jesus' six steps, and the practices and priorities of the Ephesian church, we can trace eight principles of the discipling church through the New Testament:

1. An intentional strategy
2. The Great Commission at the heart of ministry
3. Multiplication as a methodology
4. Accountability as a catalyst to obedience
5. The small group as the primary discipling vehicle
6. Apprenticeship in developing leaders
7. Leadership selection by gifts and character
8. Decentralization of ministry

As we've looked at the growth of the church, these elements have intertwined. Now let's follow each through the development of the discipling church.

An Intentional Strategy

The disciples possessed a guidance system called "the way Jesus did it." While we derive our principles from the written Word, they focused on the living Word. Remembering what they had experienced with Jesus, the leaders of the first church applied Jesus' promise: "All this I have spoken while still with you. But the Counselor, the Holy Spirit, whom the Father will send in my name, will teach you all things and will remind you of everything I have said to you" (John 14:25, 26). As God reminded them, they acted.

The apostles had a simple but firmly established guidance system. First you gather people by preaching the Good News; then you establish the core commitments presented in Acts 2:42–47:

1. To Scripture as the source of truth
2. To one another
3. To prayer
4. To praise and worship
5. To outreach

They had learned these priorities from Jesus, and the church grew.

God directly intervened in the discipling process when He provided the persecution that spread the church to Judea, Samaria, and the entire world. Sending Philip to Samaria and Peter to Cornelius, God convinced the apostles of His desire to reach the Gentiles. Further, he converted Paul and moved the center of the action to Antioch. God Himself had an intentional strategy, which He moved forward by circumstances.

God passed His strategy to Paul, who preached the Gospel, established churches, and appointed elders in the Gentile congregations. By converting people, making disciples, teaching them to obey, providing pastoral care, and developing leaders, the church obeyed Christ's commands. The healthy churches that developed reproduced and multiplied, taking the Gospel to all nations.

Strategic thinkers are few in the church ranks. Those like Paul and Barnabas plan to reach a region or group of people, develop steps to achieve their goal, and execute the plan. When the two apostles faced opposition, they adjusted; they kept going when defeated, visited churches on their way home, and appointed elders. In God's hands, people intentionally joined to strategic thinking become hammers and nails. They allow Him to stake out His territory in enemy land.

As Paul ventured out on the second journey, we see his intentions worked out. He started by planning to see the Galatian churches again and to move into Asia. Realizing the importance of maintaining ministry at all levels, he taught the existing churches, planted new churches in Macedonia, and continued with his pastoral work in Corinth. His letters to the Thessalonians demonstrate the continued need to build churches.

In Ephesus, Paul had a clear idea of what he wanted to accomplish. When his synagogue strategy went sour in three months, he took his disciples to the hall of Tyrannus without missing a beat. There he communicated the three levels of ministry: the people's priorities, the pastoral priorities, and the leadership community. All three exemplify his intentional strategies.

The initial spread of the Gospel was no haphazard thing. Every step of the way we see planning and intentional movement toward this goal. The modern-day congregation that makes intentional plans can see the same kinds of results— but they must follow the plan Jesus gave and Paul used.

The Great Commission at the Heart of Ministry

By definition, having the Great Commission at a ministry's heart means setting up disciple making as the main focus. The first church did that as they took the first step in reaching people. First-church Christians devoted themselves to disciple making, following the continued and determined

witness of the twelve, who had demonstrated their commitment to bring more and more disciples into the growing
environment. Once conversion took place, they focused on
bringing about maturity that would lead to reproduction.

The disciples had demonstrated their convictions when
they refused to leave the ministry of the Word, teaching the
church, and evangelizing the world. They would not be de-
toured from discipling; it was their calling and sat at the
heart of all they did (Acts 6:1–7).

The Great Commission lies behind God's breaking the
barriers of the church at Jerusalem. God willingly overlooked
people's fears, comforts, and the inconveniences to them.
Not even their torture and death could stop Him from sending out His people, so deep is His commitment to the expanding church. It took drastic action—persecution—to keep
the church on the edge of the Great Commission.

The first church gave its blessing to the expansion God
had begun, because they considered suffering part of the
normal way in which God worked. They had seen the cross
and could buy just about any means for getting God's work
done. The approval of the missions to the Samaritans, the
Gentiles, and the unauthorized planting of the Antioch
church testify to their faith-filled support for the Great Commission.

Make the Great Commission the engine that drives the
church, despite complaints and apologetics that would distract you. No one loves His people more than God, who
forces them to face hard tasks. No one likes to leave a comfort zone, but God prods us from our comfortable niches
with the driving force of the Great Commission.

The willingness to send out Paul and Barnabas shows
the church at Antioch's total commitment to the commission.
Though they would have found it easier to quit after being
left for dead outside Lystra, the two apostles pushed on to
over eight major cities. Their desire to keep going, their
commitment to return to churches puts starch in the men's
determination to not only win people but develop them.

When he broke with Barnabas, Paul demonstrated his passion for the task before him. He parted company with anyone whom he thought slowed down his ministry to push out to the unreached world. Like Paul, I often need to ask myself, *Where can I make the most disciples and best fulfill the Great Commission?*

As he pushes toward northern Asia we more clearly see Paul's desire to strengthen the church. When God changes the plan, sending him to Macedonia, Paul responds with quick obedience. His determination to keep on working, preaching wherever the people are, seems striking. Thrown out of one town in Macedonia, he moved on to the next. Rejected by Jews, he moved to the Gentiles. Paul never stopped dreaming, praying, and planning. When faced with human disappointments, he still kept his eyes on the Great Commission.

Powered by the desire to spread the Gospel to all nations, Paul refused to allow the Ephesian outreach to end at the city gates. Even when he lay in prison, Paul oversaw the expansion of the church. Through letters, envoys, and prayers, he worked for the Great Commission to move forward. Should the modern church be any different?

Multiplication as a Methodology

The first church had the intentional strategy of making reproducing disciples, as described in Acts 2:42–47. Guided by Acts 1:8, the twelve must have planned to send out many disciples. A reproductive congregation led to believers who reproduced the same practices wherever they went. They would start churches by preaching and would organize converts into small groups that would practice these priorities and reproduce in turn.

At the back of their minds, the twelve had always had the idea of making multiplication happen, but it didn't happen until God took a hand. The church's scattering turned reproduction into multiplication, for the apostles had trained their disciples well. Philip's Samaritans told others. The Ethiopian returned home, and tradition tells us many accepted Christ. The men of Cyrene and Cyprus preached to the Gentiles. The scattered church, Luke reports, preached wherever its disciples went. Multiplication works!

As Paul and Barnabas founded new churches, the converts took part primarily in "Come and see" activity. Because they could not stay, the two apostles appointed leaders to the fledgling churches, though as yet little "Come and follow Me" teaching had occurred. Better *some* leadership than none at all. Paul and Barnabas prayerfully appointed elders and hoped for the best.

Reproduction must occur before multiplication, and in the early stages, the new churches could not expand into the world. The first priority was to learn to reproduce on an individual scale—the rest would come with maturity, as we see in the second thrust of the mission church. Though unplanned, the mission of Timothy, Silas, and company among the Macedonian churches stands out as multiplication. Barnabas took John Mark and returned to Cyprus, to work there. Strategically Paul planned multiplication by apprenticing Timothy, Silas, Luke, Apollos, Aquila, and Priscilla, and the rest.

In this phase of the mission church, we see the strongest evidence of Paul's commitment to discipling in his letters to the Thessalonians, especially 1 Thessalonians 1:5–8. He based his prescription for the Thessalonians on what he had learned of Jesus' plan. Not only were people to accept Christ, they should move on to reproduction. This is the lifeblood of the church.

Paul did not set up these apprentices as so much window dressing. Instead of simply listening to his teachings, these disciples took on leadership roles and gave Paul input. They were the "faithful men who could teach others also" (*see* 2 Timothy 2:2). Jesus had taught to reach the world only by making disciples. In Ephesus we see how it worked on a daily basis. Paul had put all his eggs in the multiplication basket, and it held up.

Accountability as a Catalyst to Obedience

I define *accountability* as "helping people keep their commitments to God." The first church practiced this by praying for ten days in the Upper Room; they moved in with one another to encourage and train; they practiced the five priorities, shared material goods, and submitted to the apostles' judgment.

We cannot separate the roles of authority and accountability in the church; the two walk hand in hand. Ananias and Sapphira's case certainly teaches the vital role authority plays in the church. Because the church submitted to the way the twelve solved internal and external problems, the ministry flourished. Submission to authority was woven into first church's daily life. Without loving authority, the rate of growth and sheer numbers of the first church would have produced chaos. When people accepted this accountability to their leaders, they encouraged the spread of the Gospel.

Peter and John exhibited authority when they traveled to Samaria to inspect Philip's work. They found that the Samaritans had truly believed, and God gave the measure of their conversion by filling the Samaritans with the Spirit and gifting them with speaking in tongues. After the church broke through the three major barriers, the pattern of tongues signifying conversion ceased, and the gift became one given to some believers, but not all.

Peter and John returned to report their findings to the other apostles in this case, as Peter would in the case of Cornelius. Open to change and the leading of God's Spirit, the apostles accepted their evidence. But careful consideration that insured the message and methods they had learned from Jesus remained part of their accountability system.

Barnabas was sent to check out the new church in Antioch. When he reported back, bringing a financial gift to the Jerusalem church, the Antioch believers impressively demonstrated their spiritual reality.

The first journey of Paul and Barnabas testifies to their accountability. Before they left Antioch, church leaders laid hands on them, symbolizing that the elders had delegated authority to them. The elders left the details of the ministry to the evangelists, commissioning them simply to go, preach the Gospel, and report back.

After establishing a church, the evangelists appointed elders, passing on the authority again. Surely Paul and Barnabas explained the need for authority and its ramifications before they established leaders.

The early church seemed to have no doubts that serious questions should be answered by the council in Jerusalem. When the issue concerning the Gentiles required clarification, Paul, Barnabas, and the church at Antioch could not respond with authority. Strong men took their passionate opinions to Jerusalem. After discussion, James issued the decree, which was carefully communicated to Antioch and the new churches.

To obey God, the first church, mission church, and all subsequent churches need accountability. Christ had told the twelve, "Teach them to obey everything I have commanded you" (*see* Matthew 28:20). You cannot make disciples without accountability.

The modern church knows little about the positives of accountability because it knows little about discipling. When you only pay attention to a person's life-style when his actions become a church-discipline issue, he will almost always respond negatively. By ignoring the little things and pouncing on the big ones, you ask for trouble.

If you work on the little things that build faithfulness, character, and relationship, you prevent most larger problems by heading them off before they happen. Should a larger problem occur, because you have a relationship with the person, you can receive a more positive response to your correction.

In the relationships of Paul's apprentices we see accountability develop. Look, for example, at Paul and Silas. Living and working together, they became mutually accountable. Too often that word implies disciplinary action, but in reality it has a positive side, as you help one another keep daily commitments.

Paul shows the strongest accountability toward God, with his readiness to do anything He required. God held Paul accountable through encouragement in the split with Barnabas, the order to Macedonia, the order to continue preaching after the Corinthian rejection. The exhortation to encourage one another in how to live for Christ is five times more relevant in Scripture than the order to deal with difficulty. I really doubt we can maintain a consistent Christian walk without others to help us.

In Ephesus, accountability appears as common as the sun is in San Diego. It touched everything, and you could feel its presence. Upon this congregation Paul put the expectations that they would remain faithful, develop gifts, and contribute. The pastor would lead a Word-driven ministry, and all potential leaders would join the ministry community and reach full productivity.

The Ephesians held one another to their commitments. The greatest level of accountability is always based on one person's relationship with another. Unless a loving, affirming environment exists, you cannot hold anyone accountable.

The Small Group as the Primary Discipling Vehicle

From Jesus the disciples learned and practiced the house-to-house concept. With over 5,000 Christians, the Jerusalem church would have had to break members down into manageable units.

Acts 6:1–7 proves the disciples thought in management terms. They placed seven men in leadership positions. Scripture does not record how they supervised the hundreds of others, but with 5,000 to 10,000 people, they had to have hundreds of cell leaders. In mini congregations, prayer, communion, study of Scripture, worship, and outreach could find their impetus. Some system of accountability was required to stimulate their faith.

Hundreds of leaders would have had to work under

certain agreed-upon expectations. In light of their training, it would be shocking to think the twelve did not prescribe priorities (Matthew 10; Luke 10:1–24). I believe the first-church ministry was well organized. Mini-congregation leaders certainly must have formed the base of the summoned group called "all the disciples" (Acts 6:2).

Though the small group receives no mention in the mission church, the lack of church buildings and the traditions of the apostles and the first church probably indicate they existed. Later, you might say Paul, Barnabas, and John Mark formed a small group. For any community building, training, or outreach, people must be divided into manageable groups.

Before Paul reached Ephesus, you might call his small traveling band a small group. Once he got there, we know Paul ministered ". . . from house to house" (Acts 20:20). Common sense tells us that Paul must also have met with his elders and others in small-group settings. The leadership community again serves as an example of a small group. Small groups of men doubtless evangelized Asia. Considering how Jesus sent out the disciples and the mission of Paul and Barnabas, perhaps they went out in twos.

Personally I believe effective discipling must take place in a small-group setting. It provides intimacy; a variety of gifts, without an overwhelming atmosphere; and an ideal training vehicle for reproduction. It teaches well, provides accountability, and can become the launching pad for large-group activities. (For more information on small groups, *see* the Appendix.)

Apprenticeship in Developing Leaders

Apprenticeship only occurred in its most embryonic stages in the first church. The selection of the seven men indicates a willingness to delegate and a confidence that others could minister. It also shows the twelve were willing to practice what Jesus had modeled (Luke 16:10). Doubtless the house congregations had leaders whom the apostles trained in pastoring. The disciples mentioned in Acts 6:2 were probably those leaders, since the apostles could not possibly have called together 5,000 people to make such a decision. Shortly after Paul's conversion, Scripture demonstrates that within a short period of time he had his own disciples (9:25). When Peter visited Cornelius, he brought along several "brothers," who were "astonished" at what happened (10:23, 45).

When Barnabas went to Antioch, he brought along the apprentice Saul. Returning to that city, after Barnabas had taken Antioch's gift to the first church, Barnabas and Saul brought along another apprentice, John Mark (12:25).

The principle of selectivity was always at work. Developing leaders is crucial to creating a vibrant, multiplying church. The process should begin early and continue over years, allowing the apprentice to assimilate information and gain experience.

For a whole year Barnabas and Saul taught in Antioch. They must have encouraged leaders to develop gifts and roles, since leaders are mentioned in Acts 13:1–3. Because God sent Barnabas and Saul out to mission, leaving the new leaders in charge, we know the apprenticeship in Antioch had worked.

As the evangelists moved about establishing new churches, they began to implement "Come and see," "Come and follow Me," and "Come and be with Me" in successive journeys. But from the first all three principles worked simultaneously. Initial apprenticeship was informal, but it sped along the fast track.

To be successful in God's eyes, ministry must multiply, and that occurs through apprenticing. No shortcuts, only patient, hard work trains and develops leaders.

On the second journey Paul began apprenticing Silas, Timothy, and Luke. By the end of the journey he had five named apprentices and eleven other named converts. As the apostle preached in fifteen cities, over the course of four years, he planted at least nine churches and developed five to ten good, named leaders. Personally I believe he influenced hundreds of potential leaders throughout Galatia, Macedonia, and Greece. Paul's leadership community at Ephesus numbered more than thirty. Within this, he focused his attention on development.

Any church that wishes to maintain and expand priorities and practices requires a leadership community that apprentices leaders. If apprenticeship is not part of your ministry, attrition eats away at your leadership core. You will not be able to expand or maintain effectiveness, and the juice will drain from your work.

By organizing and establishing a leadership community, you can expect to keep the vision before the people and see greater creativity and ownership of your goals. A fishing pool of trained, highly motivated leaders to staff ongoing ministry and outreach will multiply your efforts. This is the fruit and work of the discipling church, so why not start now?

Leadership Selection by Gifts and Character

In the selection of Judas's replacement we see the selection process of the disciples and the qualifications needed for leadership. The man they chose had to be among the 120 (and I would be shocked if he were not one of the seventy), with a great deal of ministry experience. He was a believer who had demonstrated obedience, since he was with them at that moment. He had known Christ and witnessed His ministry—in fact they required that he had been around since John the Baptist.

When the apostles chose the seven, they asked for men filled with the Spirit and wisdom. The seven had exhibited this by their behavior; proven men of character, they possessed the administrative gifts to handle the situation. Though Luke does not expose us to many qualifications for leadership in the Jerusalem church, as the church expands we will see this principle grow as well.

As God broke the barriers of the Jerusalem church, He provided leaders directly. He chose Saul to minister to the Gentiles, without consulting man. Saul's gifts, education, and ability to commit made him God's choice. By and large, leadership would remain an interactive thing between God and the church. The first church consulted and chose Barnabas. Philip went to Samaria because of his giftedness, but Peter was sent to Cornelius as a matter of necessity. God saw to it that Peter saw the tongues in Jerusalem, Samaria, and among the Gentiles. Otherwise no one of his opinions and personality would have yielded to such changes. Even so, he had difficulty living out his new convictions. The Holy Spirit made the selection of Saul and Barnabas as Antioch's first church planters, and the church confirmed it.

Luke never records the criteria for choosing elders in the new churches. However we can safely assume the choice required more than a "holy hunch." Looking at Christ's example, in His choice of the twelve, the criteria the apostles used in selecting leaders, and Paul's letters to Timothy and Titus, we can make a strong case for objective criteria as the basis for leadership selection.

Though we do not know all the details on how Paul chose Silas, Luke, and others, we have an excellent example of Paul's criteria in Timothy. In addition, Paul's rejection of John Mark shows that he chose Silas for his task-oriented outlook and good track record.

Paul's letters to Timothy provide clear qualifications for leadership. We must assume Paul practiced these principles, probably at Ephesus. After describing nineteen qualifications for leaders, he issued Timothy a serious charge concerning the importance of such matters (1 Timothy 5:17–20).

Leadership development and selection are joined at the hip. If you do not stock the pool through leadership development, you will not have a good choice when you seek church leaders. Developed leaders are good leaders. Commit yourself to developing them, and you will benefit the church at large.

Decentralization of Ministry

Disciple making lies at the heart of the Great Commission and exists to create qualified personnel through whom church ministry can reproduce and multiply.

Making disciples was central to the thinking of the first church, where hundreds of people carried out hundreds of tasks. The apostles communicated decentralization of ministry by giving authority to the seven men and staying in Jerusalem when the church scattered. Had the twelve accompanied the scattered church, many good ministers would have remained underchallenged and underdeveloped. The preaching missions of Stephen, Philip, and others show the apostles had bestowed their blessing on the ministry of others.

When God scattered the church, He smashed institutionalism. Just as the apostles stood back and deferred to Jesus until He left, the people at the first church deferred to the apostles, who were doing miracles, until the scattering. Without decentralization, ministry could not have its maximum effect. Scattered, the church preached wherever it went, effectively carrying out the Great Commission.

Many churches see church as a place of safety from the storms of life. They believe the primary purpose of the church is care and feeding of the saints. If that were true, it would make the church no more than a way station for the selfish. But their view in no way fits with the biblical vision for the church.

The mission church portrays decentralization on a massive scale. Hundreds, possibly thousands, had turned to Christ, and the thought of leaving these people in others' care, while they returned to evangelism, must have troubled the caring Paul and Barnabas. But Paul said, ". . . He who began a good work in you will carry it on to completion until the day of Christ Jesus" (Philippians 1:6). Turning over the care of babes in Christ requires an act of faith: Spiritual parents must make this emotionally difficult decision, knowing God controls the outcome.

"Paul and Barnabas appointed elders for them in each church and, with prayer and fasting, committed them to the Lord, in whom they had put their trust" (Acts 14:23, 24). They committed the elders to the Lord, but did not commit their trust to the elders. They trusted God to watch over the church leaders. Only because of the commitment of the Lord to His church could they pass on this sacred trust to the elders. Christ promised, ". . . I will build my church . . ." (Matthew 16:18), He is the architect; we are the construction workers.

Many modern leaders do not possess a strong sense of calling that overcomes the tendency to succumb to emotions. They become swamped by doubts in situations where they have had more opportunity to train people than Paul did. Paul could not both obey his calling and stay in the new churches. He had confidence in God to care for and raise up good leadership. Good leaders have also been delivered from the cult of self-importance.

But don't equate decentralization with missionary outreach alone. Many say, "Yes, Paul *had* to decentralize, because he *had* to move on." But even in Ephesus, where he stayed for three years, he decentralized. To obey God, decentralization is a leader's nonnegotiable.

The second missionary journey provides abundant examples of decentralization. Paul's reaffirmation of the Galatian elders and churches demonstrated a commitment to local church autonomy. Though the church should be independent, like an adult, it also needs to have accountability with a larger system. By visiting the congregations, Paul established that they remained accountable to him.

When the situation demanded that Silas and Timothy remain in Macedonia, this unexpected decentralization worked because Paul had apprenticed the two men and selected them for their gifts and character. Prepared leadership made effective ministry possible.

During his eighteen months in Corinth, Paul trained many and gave responsibility to the likes of Aquila and Priscilla, who in turn discipled the powerful preacher Apollos. Wherever he went, Paul sought to create a leadership base. With the growing number of churches, the need for leaders became larger than the trained personnel. Paul had no choice but to expand his leadership base, so the ministry could continue to expand. Like him, we have a choice: Grow or die. Paul did not turn back, and neither should we.

Ephesians 4:16 provides the description of the mature corporate church: ". . . The whole body, joined and held together by every supporting ligament, grows and builds itself up in love, as each part does its work." For decentralization to become a reality, the foundation must be well laid, and that foundation is for the pastor and people to know the expectations Scripture describes and work together toward them. Creating a leadership community, identifying gifts, and training people will develop the full creativity and multiplicity of work God has for the church.

Both leaders and followers must meet scriptural expectations. Without teamwork between congregation and pastor, it cannot be done. The essence of a discipling church is full employment of congregational members in a wide variety of ministry. Are you willing to invest your life in making yours a discipling church?

Appendix

Developing a Leadership Community
Randall K. Knutson

Introduction

Today, because of the confusion about disciple making, the church often faces accusations that it is unable to make disciples, when in fact the opposite is true. What do we mean when we talk about disciples? Let's begin by clarifying some terms.

All people who place their faith in Christ as the atonement for their sins are Christ's *disciples*. Once they have made this profession of faith, God commands them to move on and grow in it. Such a process involves the discipling of believers to love, unity, and spiritual maturity, and it never ends for any believer. From children to senior adults, all are expected to continue on their spiritual journey. Confusion comes when we teach that discipleship is a program, not a process! We can most clearly see this process in a church structure, because it involves the full life cycle, with people of all ages.

Making disciples refers to leading people to faith in Christ, the commanded task of His church. *Discipling* means taking believers and moving them on in faith, so they begin to mature and employ their gifts in the body of Christ. Thus they fulfill their calling in life to start with their own Jerusalem. Discipling includes all groups in the church that process people to the next step of spiritual maturation. The church should be viewed as a holistic discipling unit, a living, organic body that moves people on in their relationship to Christ and in service.

When Christ discipled, He was God-man. Full deity rested in Him, along with all the gifts of the Spirit. In John 14 he told us His leaving would be to our advantage, since it would let the Spirit impart gifts to accomplish His Great Commission. Now, not as individuals, but as a church, we disciple.

A church becomes a mature, discipling church when it reaches the "Come and be with Me" or reproductive stage, on a corporate and intentional level. In most churches this takes place, at best, on a small, unintentional scale. The distinctive of the discipling church is that it intentionally develops a leadership community. If you want your church to follow the tradition of Jesus, the first church, and the mission church, to become a discipling church, you must intentionally equip your leadership community.

This appendix illustrates *a way*, not *the way*, to structure a discipling church. I have divided it into three parts:

PART I: LEADERSHIP COMMUNITY will help you understand the basic components of the leadership community.

PART II: HOW TO RUN A CELL-BASED CHURCH will examine how small groups are set up to decentralize pastoral care from within the leadership community.

PART III: STRUCTURING YOUR SMALL GROUPS will show how to instruct apprentices so that they can move from successful small-group planning to prayerful completion of the basic tasks.

Finally I have provided a list of additional resources for a discipling church.

PART I
Leadership Community

To establish your own leadership community, you will need to carry out nine functions of the community:

1. Illustrating a cell-based church structure
2. Describing a leadership community
3. Structuring a leadership community
4. Developing expanding networks of small groups (cells)
5. Selecting apprentices
6. Examining an apprentice's covenant
7. Reviewing a job description for a small group leader
8. Reviewing a job description for a supervisory huddle leader
9. Creating evangelistic fishing pools

A Church-Centered Disciple-Making Plan

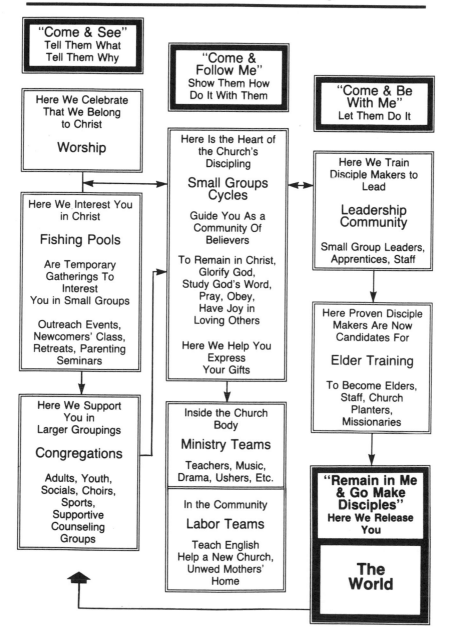

"Come & See"
Tell Them What
Tell Them Why

"Come & Follow Me"
Show Them How
Do It With Them

"Come & Be With Me"
Let Them Do It

Here We Celebrate
That We Belong
to Christ

Worship

Here Is the Heart of
the Church's
Discipling

Small Groups
Cycles

Guide You As a
Community Of
Believers

Here We Train
Disciple Makers to
Lead

Leadership
Community

Small Group Leaders,
Apprentices, Staff

Here We Interest You
in Christ

Fishing Pools

Are Temporary
Gatherings To
Interest
You in Small Groups

Outreach Events,
Newcomers' Class,
Retreats, Parenting
Seminars

To Remain in Christ,
Glorify God,
Study God's Word,
Pray, Obey,
Have Joy in
Loving Others

Here We Help You
Express
Your Gifts

Here Proven Disciple
Makers Are Now
Candidates For

Elder Training

To Become Elders,
Staff, Church
Planters,
Missionaries

Here We Support
You in
Larger Groupings

Congregations

Adults, Youth,
Socials, Choirs,
Sports,
Supportive
Counseling
Groups

Inside the Church
Body

Ministry Teams

Teachers, Music,
Drama, Ushers, Etc.

In the Community

Labor Teams

Teach English
Help a New Church,
Unwed Mothers'
Home

"Remain in Me
& Go Make
Disciples"
Here We Release
You

The
World

ILLUSTRATING A CELL-BASED CHURCH STRUCTURE

The following chart illustrates how we employed a holistic discipling process, through small groups, to mobilize a congregation to use its gifts.

DESCRIBING A LEADERSHIP COMMUNITY

The leadership community is the place for active small-group leaders to gain personal support, expand their vision, develop ministry skills, and intern new apprentices into active leadership.

Leadership Community	A congregational unit of leadership from all ministry activities that involve small groups of people; it meets for dinner, worship, prayer, direction, and support for personal growth.
Active Small Group	We have decentralized the pastoral care of our church and given pastoring responsibilities to the various small groups (for example, music/worship ensembles, drama teams, intervention groups, junior- and senior-high sponsors, and all small groups from the youth, men's, women's, singles, and couples studies).
Leaders	The leadership community is for those who are currently in or about to enter into the active leadership level of service in a small group.

Personal Support	This is a time for the shepherds of the church to become sheep and be cared for.
Expand Vision	A place to express our core values, paint the big picture, and plan for future growth in ministry.
Develop Skills	Time is set aside to train and prepare people to use their leadership gifts for effective service.
Intern Apprentices	A place to bring newly identified apprentices into entry-level leadership, to nurture them in the use of their giftedness.

STRUCTURING A LEADERSHIP COMMUNITY

Our leadership community meets every other week. We decided to meet every other week because of the Nehemiah principle, which states that it only takes one month for a person to lose his vision. So if a leader misses one meeting, he or she can still make contact with the leadership community within a thirty-day period of time.

Here is how our evening works:

1. We bring in pizza and eat together (fifteen minutes). We choose an early evening time on Monday night, from 5:30–7:30, to meet. It is a tightly packed two hours, so our people can get home early. This time works best for both our men and women, since sitters are easier to access, and husband and wife can come together, if they desire. Placing it early means it does not feel like another night out, and family needs can still be met.
2. We have a worship time together and prayer for various topics provided by our worship team (fifteen minutes).
3. The pastor leads the leadership community with thirty to forty-five minutes of vision casting, prayer, worship, and

encouragement for those who are living out our core values.

4. We divide up by affinity into small huddles of three to five people for personal prayer, reporting on groups' progress, and troubleshooting (forty-five minutes).

5. We periodically plan a retreat or special time to conduct our fishing-pool strategy session or training time, to plan how to introduce our new groups to newcomers during specific outreach events sponsored by the church at large.

6. Titles for our leaders within the leadership community are as follows:

SMALL-GROUP LEADER	Shepherds ten people and develops one apprentice.
HUDDLE LEADER	Coaches three to five small group leaders.
APPRENTICE	Recruits a small group from his existing group and from fishing-pool events.
COORDINATOR	Administrates leadership community and new fishing-pool events.

DEVELOPING EXPANDING NETWORKS OF HEALTHY SMALL GROUPS

The following diagram illustrates the kind of group dynamics a leadership community develops. All our small groups unite together, from every angle of the church, and bring their apprentices.

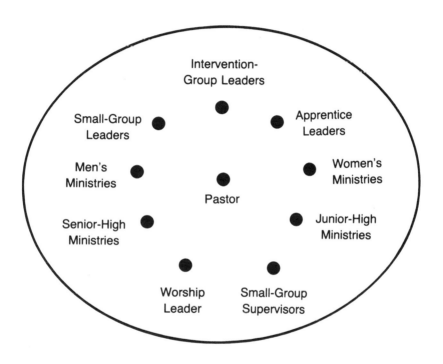

The benefits of networking these groups together are:

1. It increases communication between the different areas.
2. You can think out how to win entire families to Christ.
3. It is an effective way to expand new groups.
4. You get clear feedback of ministry effects.

The following diagram illustrates how we divided up in our leadership-community time.

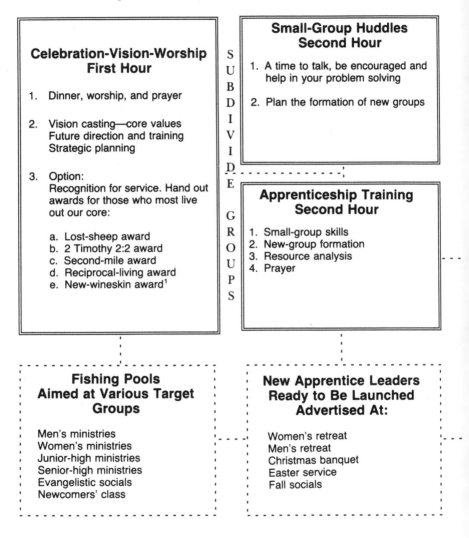

**Celebration-Vision-Worship
First Hour**

1. Dinner, worship, and prayer

2. Vision casting—core values
   Future direction and training
   Strategic planning

3. Option:
   Recognition for service. Hand out
   awards for those who most live
   out our core:

   a. Lost-sheep award
   b. 2 Timothy 2:2 award
   c. Second-mile award
   d. Reciprocal-living award
   e. New-wineskin award[1]

S U B D I V I D E G R O U P S

**Small-Group Huddles
Second Hour**

1. A time to talk, be encouraged and
   help in your problem solving

2. Plan the formation of new groups

**Apprenticeship Training
Second Hour**

1. Small-group skills
2. New-group formation
3. Resource analysis
4. Prayer

**Fishing Pools
Aimed at Various Target
Groups**

Men's ministries
Women's ministries
Junior-high ministries
Senior-high ministries
Evangelistic socials
Newcomers' class

**New Apprentice Leaders
Ready to Be Launched
Advertised At:**

Women's retreat
Men's retreat
Christmas banquet
Easter service
Fall socials

SELECTING APPRENTICES

1. Description of an Apprentice. One bound by a commitment to develop Christian character and ministry skills under the guiding influence of a trained disciple maker.

2. Qualifications for Apprentices. Apprentices are willing to join the leadership community and submit to the training process provided by a small-group leader. They must demonstrate a variety of attributes and aptitudes:

a. They must have leadership skills appropriate for the job.
b. They must aspire to join the leadership community.
c. Their hearts must burn for spiritual things.
d. They must be spiritually gifted for leadership.
e. They must be teachable and attractive to others.
f. There must not be any disqualifying weaknesses or emotional immaturity.
g. They must be able to gather a group around them.
h. They must be able to work through others and facilitate a group to minister to others.

3. Procedure for Entering Our Leadership Community. Before an apprentice joins the community, leaders take the following steps:

a. Pray and make a list of potential apprentices.
b. Small-group leader clears the potential candidate with his huddle supervisor, to see if the eight qualifications for apprenticeship are there.
c. Once given permission, the small-group leader sets up a meeting and goes over the commitment for an apprentice.
d. Have the potential apprentice read the article on the leadership community and visit Monday-night group.
e. Once an apprentice decides to join the leadership community, he or she signs the covenant sheet for apprentices, attends an orientation meeting, and is assigned a huddle leader. The huddle leader is decided upon by which group the small-group leader is in. No huddle will

EXAMINING AN APPRENTICE COVENANT

Apprentice Covenant

1. I desire to be part of the leadership community.
2. I desire to be trained in deeper Christian life-style and ministry skills for future leadership.
3. I am willing to submit to the projects and environmental culture of the leadership community. This includes:
   a. Doing my ministry assignments.
   b. Attending any special seminars or workshops designed for my development.
   c. Regularly supporting church functions.
4. I will make our meetings a top priority in my schedule and will phone in whenever I have a conflict or will be late to a meeting.
5. I commit to stay in the leadership community as long as I have ministry responsibilities.
6. I will begin a new group after my training.

After reading these expectations I feel unworthy yet challenged to attempt what you have asked. I have prayed about this commitment to the leadership community and feel God is leading me/us to become a member of this leadership team.

I desire to grow in my relationship to Christ, my love for others, and in my leadership skills. Therefore, before God and the leadership community, I agree to focus my efforts to comply with these expectations.

I give you permission, as my friend and a loving guide for my spiritual well-being, to confront me whenever I fall short of this covenant.

Name   _____

Small-group leader _____

Date   _____

be greater than five people. If a new huddle is to be formed, apprentices stay with the small-group leader in the division, as a rule.

4. Outline for an Orientation Breakfast Meeting. Once an apprentice indicates willingness to become part of the leadership community, schedule an hour-long breakfast meeting in which you can discuss the specifics of the commitment involved.

Fifteen Minutes	Coffee.
Thirty Minutes	Review leadership community article of purpose, objectives, schedule, requirements, and covenant.
Fifteen minutes	Question-and-answer time. Give the potential apprentice two weeks to return a signed covenant.

FISHING POOLS AND REPRODUCING CARE GROUPS

Carl George, of the Charles E. Fuller Institute for Church Growth, first coined the expression "fishing pools." George observes that the people who join a church or small group will do so primarily for relational reasons. An affinity to similar people, needs, or life-style is usually the reason. In this model, we developed our programming to gather new people and fold them into small groups. Fishing pools are designed sources for new small-group leaders to fill their groups.

The Definition of a Fishing Pool. A fishing pool is an intentional outreach event developed to draw in new people, identify their affinities, and interest them in new small groups that are about to start.

1. Fishing-Pool Agenda. The fishing pool has four specific aims:

REVIEWING A JOB DESCRIPTION FOR A
SMALL-GROUP LEADER

Job Description—Small-Group Leader

1. Create an Environment for Personal Growth. Organize your small-group meetings to:

    a. Apply God's Word so it addresses your people's life-styles.
    b. Build supportive and mutually accountable relationships.
    c. Worship God for who He is and what He has done.
    d. Pray and intercede for others and God's work in the world.
    e. Invite your extended family to join you.

2. Work Through Others to Care for Your Group. Pastoral care takes place two ways:

    a. LOVE Coach the group members to use their spiritual gifts with one another as a team as well as their extended families.
    b. SERVE Help them sharing and be "good news" so that people move toward becoming Christ's disciples and into the church.

3. Oversee Your Group's Progress. What do we require of you?

    a. Develop a prayer journal for all the people in your small group.
    b. Write out your own lesson plan each week, keyed to the needs of your group.
    c. Fill out small-group leader's worksheets and give them to your huddle leader.
    d. Faithfully attend church and the leadership community activities.

4. Reproduce Yourself. The litmus test for your leadership is how well you reproduce new apprentices. Train an apprentice leader who will begin another group each year.

a. Identifying specific affinity or target groups.
b. Reaching out and gathering new people.
c. Accomplishing a stated purpose.
d. Allowing apprentices to fill their groups.

2. Examples of Various Fishing Pools

a. Newcomers' class
b. Women's coffees
c. Parenting seminar
d. Women's or men's retreats
e. Marriage-enrichment weekend
f. Sports teams
g. Evangelistic Bible studies
h. Camping trips
i. Service projects to the poor and oppressed
j. Marketplace Bible studies

3. Fishing-Pool Design. All fishing-pool events run on the premises:

a. Use table-group exercise with apprentices who are about to begin a new group. Mix people up during the exercises so that everyone interacts with apprentices. Allow people to choose whom they feel most comfortable with then.
b. The remaining time is spent in table groups that are facilitated by apprentice leaders. The table-group activities are highly relational and allow people to meet others easily and identify common interests.
c. Participants are given the opportunity to meet and work with several different apprentices. Our goal is to give the opportunity for the right people to bond together and create the potential for new small groups.
d. The apprentices are preparing to launch their own groups after events like the marriage-enrichment seminar, newcomers' class, sports teams, and so on. While at

REVIEWING A JOB DESCRIPTION FOR A HUDDLE LEADER

Job Description—Huddle Leader

1. Troubleshoot Small Group's Problems. The huddle leader uses problem-solving techniques to:

    a.   Help small-group leaders formulate goals and plans. Monitor the implementation process. Encourage and affirm small-group effectiveness and reproduction.

    b.   Attend each small group every third to sixth meeting and personally debrief the performance of the group.

    c.   Help leaders to discern group and individual needs. Ask probing questions to enable leaders to identify priorities and determine the next steps to be taken.

    d.   Guide leaders to facilitate the use of spiritual gifts in their groups.

2. Shepherd Small-Group Leaders. In ministering to those under his care, a huddle leader will need to:

    a.   Develop a prayer ministry for each leader he supervises.

    b.   Spend extended time in prayer to determine agendas for ministry-community huddles.

    c.   Build personal relationships with every small-group leader he supervises. (Maximum is five.)

    d.   Utilize the alternate weeks to make regular individual contacts outside the ministry community, to offer encouragement, plan, and guide growth, as needed.

    e.   Schedule periodic planning times with small-group leaders (at least one a quarter). Follow up small-group leaders who miss the leadership community.

3. Cultivate Apprentice Leaders. To prepare new leaders, the huddle leader will want to:

    a.   Help small-group leaders identify and invest in potential leaders. Meet with potential small-group apprentices and give vision for future ministry possibilities.

    b.   Approve and invite potential small-group leaders to orientation meetings in the ministry community. Follow up apprentices in the launching of their groups. Assist small-group leaders in identifying and encouraging others to use their gifts.

    c.   Multiply himself by developing someone from his huddle who can serve as a supervisor.

these events, the apprentices are seeking to build new relationships and create a network from which they will draw their groups' members.

Divide your weekend or weekly meeting sessions into two parts. Design the first part to provide for a continual mixing of people. Look for affinity. Who likes whom? Who wants to be together? During the second part, intentionally place people in huddles by affinity and keep them in those groupings for the remainder of the seminar.

When the event ends, potential for deeper relationships is more possible. Offer a small-group orientation meeting for upcoming groups. Follow up your new contacts.

Apprentices use the newly acquired network to recruit people for their upcoming small groups. The networking process goes on and on and on!

PART II
How to Run a Cell-Based Church

This section will examine how small groups are set up to decentralize our pastoral care from our leadership community. In this section we will:

1. Explore a healthy small-group cycle
2. Illustrate a four-stage small-group cycle
3. Study a healthy-group-cycle chart
4. Review a personal-development matrix
5. Outline the makeup of a nine- to eighteen-month small-group cycle

A HEALTHY GROUP CYCLE

1. Get-Acquainted Group Study. This provides support for one another: The group-building stage, or what we call our courtship stage, is designed for getting acquainted by building the feeling of closeness and spiritual oneness and experiencing real Christian community.

A FOUR-STAGE SMALL-GROUP CYCLE
Adapted From and for Use With Serendipity Materials.

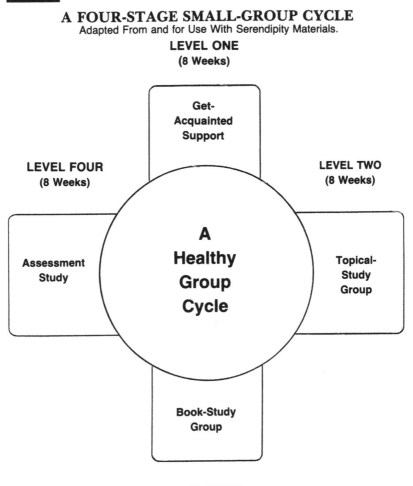

LEVEL ONE
(8 Weeks)

LEVEL FOUR
(8 Weeks)

LEVEL TWO
(8 Weeks)

Get-Acquainted Support

A Healthy Group Cycle

Assessment Study

Topical-Study Group

Book-Study Group

LEVEL THREE
(13 Weeks)

a. During this stage the group leader assesses the maturity level of the group.

b. The selection of a resource plan is made with the coordinator of new groups, during leadership-community meetings.

2. Topical Group Study. We begin with a good diet of Bible study. More challenging methods are explored. The type of

Bible study should fit the developmental growth of the group. That is:

a. FOR BEGINNERS' GROUPS: Use simple, relational forms of study designed for group building and spiritual formation.
b. FOR CONTINUING GROUPS: Use deeper Bible study that challenges the group to wrestle with its faith and with its life together as a group.
c. FOR MATURE, GRADUATE-LEVEL GROUPS: Use lots of options to challenge the group to explore not only its faith but also its mission and calling as it seeks to obey the Great Commission.

3. Book-Analysis Study. The purpose or task/mission is to learn to reach out to others in love by sharing Christ with "hurting" people who need support and love in order to achieve one of these goals:

a. Draw them into the community of the group.
b. Foster new healing communities, as the first-century Christians in the early church.

4. Assessment for next fall. Release members for their next calling.

a. EVALUATION: Ask the question, What is the next step in my career, family life, and spiritual life for next fall?
b. ASSESSMENT: Personality, gift, work style, and passions for a strategic next step are examined. Service needs in our church are studied; networking and referrals are made to appropriate leadership, based on passion and interest.
c. FEEDBACK: Tell a story to the small group, to help determine life goals and direction.
d. GRADUATION CEREMONY: All groups disband at the same time, and members shuffle into new groups. Summer is used to prepare leadership for fall.
e. RELEASE MEMBERS TO RECYCLE INTO OTHER NEW GROUPS: Phase out a group by easing its weekly meeting times to once-a-month reunions (set, for example, on Sunday af-

ternoons), so group members have time to adjust to the
change and develop the need to find new types of groups.

Material in the Above Section Adapted From And For Use With *Serendipity*
Materials

THE MAKEUP OF A NINE- TO
EIGHTEEN-MONTH SMALL-GROUP CYCLE

1. The following material should be considered when developing a four-phase group plan for a one- or two-year
   schedule.

   a. Orientation of Group. Remind small group members
      that:
      i.   Healthy affinity groups have a specific target.
      ii. An escalator clause for accountability is neces-
           sary.
      iii. There is a built-in goal to launch other groups.
   b. The nine- to eighteen-month cycle runs for nine
      months and coincides with the local school calendar
      year.
   c. Apprentices participate in one of our small groups
      and go through training in the leadership commu-
      nity before they start their small group.
   d. Groups will be started with a specific target group in
      mind. Such as:

      Mothers of preschool-age children
      Young singles
      Parents of teens
      Men's small groups at office locations
      Couples with junior-high-age children
      Couples with young children
      Marriage enrichment
      New believers
      Ten-step program
      Overcomers group—addiction issues

A HEALTHY-GROUP-CYCLE CHART

Get Acquainted 8 Weeks	Topical 1–2 Semesters	Book Study 1–2 Semesters	Assessment 8 Weeks
LEVEL ONE	LEVEL TWO	LEVEL THREE	LEVEL FOUR
		PURPOSE	
SUPPORT			GRADUATION
		BIBLE	
Building Community Life in the Group	Digging Into the Issues of Faith & Life-style	Beginning to Study Books of the Bible	Assessing Gifts & Interests for the Next Step in Group or Church Life

Adapted From Lyman Coleman's *Serendipity Small Group Training*

A PERSONAL-DEVELOPMENT MATRIX

These are the preestablished topics and skills the pastor feels he wants his people to learn as they go through a small-group cycle. Regardless of their topics, all groups practice the same items for their personal development. This matrix is used by leadership to measure if they are accomplishing what God has called them to.

Personal-Development Matrix

	Get Acquainted (8 Weeks) LEVEL ONE	Topical Study (8 Weeks) LEVEL TWO	Book Study (13 Weeks) LEVEL THREE	Assessment (8 Weeks) LEVEL FOUR
PRAYER	Conversational prayer	Half day in prayer	Intercessory prayer	Journal-keeping prayer
SUPPORT	Meals, reciprocal living, & social events	Meals, reciprocal living, & social events	Meals, reciprocal living, & social events	Meals, reciprocal living, & social events
WORD	Relational study	Topical study	Book-analysis study	Assessment study
WITNESS	Enhancing your witness Individual plan: personal story	Enhancing your witness Group plan: inviting others	Enhancing your witness Church plan: Gospel tract	Enhancing your witness Service project: to helpless

PART III
Structuring Small Groups

Healthy small groups don't just happen by accident; they are carefully planned to happen! Successful small-group planning involves prayerful completion of the following basic tasks:

1. Defining what you mean by a small group
2. Clarifying your aim
3. Focusing your goals
4. Sharing what you want your small-group members to know
5. Identifying what you want your small-group members to learn
6. Dreaming of what you want your small-group members to become
7. Structuring your small-group life as a way of life, all your life
8. Opening groups for outreach
9. Introducing your success indicators

ELEMENTS OF A SMALL GROUP

1. What Do We Mean by a Small Group? A small group is an intentional gathering of three to fourteen people who meet on a regular basis, with the common purpose of inviting the people they love to join them in discovering and growing in the adventure of a Christ-honoring life-style at work, in family life, and with extended family members.

a. Each group has its own goals and objectives, which are spelled out in simple ground rules. The small-group leader designs his or her group's schedule to coincide with the local school calendar year.

b. Authentic Christian community is more likely to be developed where there is the care and support of a cluster of three to fourteen people.

c. We encourage our groups to meet weekly, but some groups will meet on a regular biweekly or monthly basis.

d. Our common purposes are to worship Christ as our Lord and Master; to minister to one another; to unite as disciples of Christ, with a common cause; and to prepare for our mission to the world around us.

e. Our groups are open, so that you can invite the people you love who do not know where they are with God but are open to finding out and those who are already committed to Jesus Christ but desire the help of others' experience and support.

f. We believe that small groups are the best vehicle to help you learn about Christ's love, overcome life's obstacles, and experience new accomplishments. Why not try one and see for yourself?

g. We encourage you to stretch, dream, and take risks in setting personal goals for expressing your gifts at work, at home, in your community, and with Christ Himself.

h. The word *life-style* is all-inclusive—one that prays that the love of God will so control your life that you will align yourself with His purposes and receive His power and inspiration for making God-honoring changes in your attitudes and actions at work, in your home, and with your extended family.

i. Your extended family is comprised of those people who live within a reasonable driving distance of your home and who are not presently in Christ or a local church (such as, friends, neighbors, or work associates).

2. Small-Group Aim. The small group has the aim of helping our people take another step in developing a Christ-honoring life-style where they live, work, and play.

3. Small-Group Goals. To achieve our aims, we identify six group goals:

a. To decentralize our care and support.
b. To love our work associates, friends, and neighbors in word and deed.
c. To invite others into our lives and the events of the church, with the intention of making well-incorporated disciples.
d. To identify giftedness, develop it, and empower it to its logical fruition.
e. To develop apprentices as small-group leaders for future leadership roles.
f. To seek creative expression in new ministries as our people grow and develop their giftedness.

4. What Do We Want Our People to Know? We want them to know how to:

a. Worship their heavenly Father and enjoy a vital prayer life in their own relationship with Christ.
b. Study the Word of God, using a variety of resources that will help deepen their understanding of God's Word.
c. Love in word and deed, not only believers, but also their work associates, friends, and neighbors so that they can introduce them to Christ and to other believers.

d. Live out a God-honoring work ethic with their employers, employees, and the customers they serve.

e. Utilize our church family as their team for loving their extended families and inviting them to share in the Good News of Jesus Christ with us.

f. Minister to people by praying for those in their lives who need their support and spiritual nurture.

g. Use their distinct abilities, strengths, and gifts at work, with their families, and with other hurting people.

h. Access ongoing resources for future group life or ministry.

5. What Do We Want Our People to Do? We want them to:

a. Give attendance at group meetings first priority and only exit at natural breaks.

b. Participate by preparing the lessons before they come.

c. Invite new people to every meeting, as long as they understand the ground rules.

d. Intentionally open their extended family and provide loving support for the rest of the group and the friends they invite to the group.

e. Live up to an agreed-upon covenant (representative of the group's location on the small-group matrix) and start new groups as they share their faith.

f. Give permission to the members of the group to call upon one another for encouragement and prayer during times of need, even in the middle of the night.

g. Apply the principles they study in God's Word to their work, play, and friendships.

6. What Do We Want Our People to Become? We want them to grow holistically in:

a. THEIR SPIRITUAL LIFE: As our small-group members discover what He has revealed about Himself and His purpose for their lives in Jesus Christ, they are challenged to respond in both faith and commitment.

b. THEIR RELATIONSHIP TO THEIR FAMILIES AND OTHERS: To seek deeper levels of maturity and understanding for their families and others and the uniqueness of God's purposes for each person in their lives.

c. THEIR RELATIONSHIP TO THEIR CAREER: Group members gain a new appreciation and insights for God's providential work and begin to see themselves as ethical stewards who are to minister for Him at their workplaces.

7. Clarifying the Basics. We want to ground our people in the basics of:

a. PRAYER: We help them learn to set aside the time and reduce their personal RPMs from 10,000 to 5,000 so that they can enjoy conversational prayer, half days in prayer, meaningful intercession, and journal keeping.

b. FELLOWSHIP AND LOVING SUPPORT: This includes ministries such as:

    i.   Someone to call when hurting, regardless of the time of day
    ii. Providing meals for the sick
    iii. Sending cards of encouragement
    iv. Baby-sitting for one another's children
    v.   Eating and playing together as a group
    vi. Sharing what's happening in one anothers' lives
    vii. Celebrating the ordinances together

c. THE WORD OF GOD: Introduce people to the Serendipity inductive study system, which practically applies God's Word to work, family, and friend relationships.

d. THEIR SERVICE: Enhance their skills for loving and caring for one another, for reaching out as a group to others in their networks by using the strength of one another's giftedness, and by creating special activities to help incorporate them into our church's loving support system.

8. Structuring Your Small-Group Life as a Way of Life, All Your Life. So that people will continue to move toward the profile of John 15 for the rest of their lives.

This profile focuses on believers' glorifying God in their work ethics, family life, and recreational relationships by:

REMAINING in prayer and communion with God by meditating upon His Word at regular intervals each week.

BEARING FRUIT in their words and deeds as they develop an ethical, God-honoring life-style.

OBEYING God's leading by striving to make the greatest contribution to people possible in light of the resources and responsibilities God has given them.

LIVING JOYOUSLY no matter what they experience, because they are doing what God's Word wants them to do.

LOVING others and helping them in their spiritual, physical, and emotional needs.

9. Success Indicators. What we measure to keep us on track:

a. WEB FACTOR: Who is God laying on my heart to add to my prayer list?

b. AFFINITY FACTOR: Who is responding to my love? Why?

c. PROXIMITY FACTOR: What activities can I do to deepen my relationships with those at work, home, and so on?

d. LOVE FACTOR: Whom have I had in my home? What notes, cards, and gifts have I sent to others?

e. COST FACTOR: Is there anything God is asking me to do right now that I'm not willing to do?

f. FRIENDSHIP FACTOR: What do I notice about the questions and needs of my friends? I need your help in_____?

g. STRESS RECEPTIVITY FACTOR: Who around me is under stress and in pain? Is there anything I/we can do to help them?

h. PRAYER FACTOR: With whom have I prayed lately?

i. TEAM FACTOR: Who in my church or group will I introduce to my friends? When? How?

j. DECLARATION FACTOR: How am I declaring my love for Christ—by symbols, actions, prayer, or words?

k. INTIMACY FACTOR: What has God shown me about Himself this week? In what areas do I feel He wants me to grow?

l. STEWARDSHIP FACTOR: In light of the resources and responsibilities God has given me, what am I doing at my place of employment to make the greatest contribution possible to the lives of other people?[2]

ADDITIONAL RESOURCES

Bender, Edgar J. *Curriculum Study Guide* for use with *Jesus Christ Disciplemaker* (Minneapolis, Minn.: Church Ministries Department, The Evangelical Free Church of America, 1988). A good resource for a Sunday-school class, small-group Bible study, Sunday-evening training session, or special church-membership class.

Hull, Bill. *The Disciple Making Pastor* (Old Tappan, N. J.: Fleming H. Revell, 1988). An excellent tool to help pastors and church boards work through the biblical issues involved in developing a discipling strategy.

Knutson, Randall K. *Curriculum Study Guide* for use with *The Disciple Making Pastor* (Minneapolis, Minn.: Church Ministries Department, The Evangelical Free Church of America, 1988). A practical and helpful resource. A must for pastors and church leaders who are developing a discipling strategy.

Hull, Bill. *Jesus Christ Disciplemaker* (Old Tappan, N. J.: Fleming H. Revell, 1990.) A journey through the Gospels traces Christ's discipling strategy to help introduce basic dis-

cipling principles into your church. (The Appendix is a special pastoral study guide on how to introduce a biblical
philosophy to your church.)

Disciple Making Ministries, a San Diego, California,
based ministry, conducts conferences and seminar/
workshops for pastors and key church leaders to help them
place disciple making at the very heart of their churches'
ministries. DMM also provides various resources for pastors
and their leadership.

*For more information concerning seminars and resources, contact
Disciple Making Ministries, P.O. Box 28172, San Diego, CA
92128, 619-487-0100.*

SOURCE NOTES

Introduction

1. This is a summary of the study reported in James Hunter, *Evangelism: The Coming Generation* (Chicago, Ill.: University of Chicago Press, 1987), 203–207.

Chapter 1

1. This is made clear in G. W. Bromily, *The Theological Dictionary of the New Testament* (Grand Rapids, Mich.: William B. Eerdmans Pub. Co., 1967), 457–459.

2. Ibid., 441.

3. Michael Wilkins, *The Concept of Disciple in Matthew's Gospel as Reflected in the Use of the Term Mathetes* (Leiden: E. J. Brill, 1988), 160.

4. Robert Coleman, *The Master Plan of Discipleship* (Old Tappan, N. J.: Fleming H. Revell Co., 1987), 99.

5. Paraphrased from Wilkins, *Concept of Disciple*. It should be noted that Wilkins does not agree with this thesis and very effectively argues against it.

6. I highly recommend reading Dr. Michael J. Wilkins's articles, published in the appendix of the yet-to-be-published *The Anchor Bible Dictionary* (Garden City, N. Y.: Doubleday). Volumes forthcoming.

7. My book, *Jesus Christ Disciplemaker* (Old Tappan, N. J.: Fleming H. Revell Co., 1984) is dedicated to the belief that Jesus modeled disciple making.

Chapter 2

1. I have covered this text from the pastor's viewpoint in some detail in my book *The Disciple Making Pastor* (Old Tappan, N. J.: Fleming H. Revell Co., 1988).

Chapter 3

1. For more information on these steps, see my book *Jesus Christ Disciplemaker* (Old Tappan, N. J.: Fleming H. Revell Co., 1984).

Chapter 4

1. E. M. Bounds, *A Treasury of Prayer*, comp. Leonard Ravenhill (Minneapolis, Minn.: Bethany Fellowship, 1961), 99.

Chapter 6

1. Michael Green, *Evangelism in the Early Church* (Grand Rapids, Mich.: William B. Eerdmans Pub. Co., 1970), 274.

Chapter 7

1. Michael Green, *Evangelism in the Early Church* (Grand Rapids, Mich.: William B. Eerdmans Pub. Co., 1970), 194.
2. Ibid., 195.
3. William L. Coleman, *The Pharisees' Guide to Total Holiness* (Minneapolis, Minn.: Bethany House, 1977), 24.
4. Ibid., 26, 27.

Chapter 8

1. John Sterling, *An Atlas of Acts* (Old Tappan, N. J.: Fleming H. Revell Co., 1966), 10–14.

Chapter 9

1. Michael J. Wilkins, to appear in the yet-to-be-published *Anchor Bible Dictionary* (Garden City, N. Y.: Doubleday). Volumes forthcoming.

2. Ibid.

3. Ibid. Wilkins's treatment of New Testament words related to the discipling process is extremely valuable. His book *The Concept of Disciple in Matthew's Gospel* (Leiden: E. J. Brill, 1988), has proved a Godsend to my study.

4. Ibid.

Chapter 10

1. Michael Green, *Evangelism in the Early Church* (Grand Rapids, Mich.: William B. Eerdmans Pub. Co., 1970), 206.

2. For a fuller treatment of the issue of leadership from the leadership angle, see my work *The Disciple Making Pastor* (Old Tappan, N. J.: Fleming H. Revell Co., 1988).

3. Additional information on the nature of change may be found in Ephesians 4:17–32. *See also* the parallel passage in Colossians 3:12–17.

4. For textual detail *see* my book *Right Thinking, Insights on Spiritual Growth* (Colorado Springs, Colo.: NavPress, 1985).

Chapter 11

1. Walter Lock, *The International Critical Commentary* (Edinburgh: T & T Clark, 1924), 110, 111.

2. Bill Hull, *The Disciple Making Pastor* (Old Tappan, N. J.: Fleming H. Revell Co., 1988), 238–247.

3. For more information on how 2 Timothy 2:2 teaches this, *see* ibid., 135–140.

Chapter 12

1. Michael Green, *Evangelism in the Early Church* (Grand Rapids, Mich.: William B. Eerdmans Pub. Co., 1970), 206.

2. Ibid., 204.

3. Ibid., 205.

4. For more concerning the six-step teaching method of Christ and the training phases He used, see my books *Jesus Christ Disciplemaker* (Old Tappan, N. J.: Fleming H. Revell Co., 1984), and *The Disciple Making Pastor* (Old Tappan, N. J.: Fleming H. Revell Co., 1988).

Appendix

1. These award names are from Robert E. Logan, *Beyond Church Growth* (Old Tappan, N. J.: Fleming H. Revell Co., 1989), 156.

2. Factor names are from Win Arn, *The Master's Plan for Making Disciples* (Monrovia, Calif.: Church Growth, 1982).